# Ethical Research with Children

# Ethical Research with Children

## Untold Narratives and Taboos

Sarah Richards, Jessica Clark and Allison Boggis
*University Campus Suffolk, UK*

First published 2015 by
PALGRAVE MACMILLAN

Palgrave Macmillan in the UK is an imprint of Macmillan Publishers Limited, registered in England, company number 785998, of Houndmills, Basingstoke, Hampshire RG21 6XS.

Palgrave Macmillan in the US is a division of St Martin's Press LLC, 175 Fifth Avenue, New York, NY 10010.

Palgrave Macmillan is the global academic imprint of the above companies and has companies and representatives throughout the world.

Palgrave® and Macmillan® are registered trademarks in the United States, the United Kingdom, Europe and other countries.

ISBN 978–1–137–35130–2

This book is printed on paper suitable for recycling and made from fully managed and sustained forest sources. Logging, pulping and manufacturing processes are expected to conform to the environmental regulations of the country of origin.

A catalogue record for this book is available from the British Library.

A catalog record for this book is available from the Library of Congress.

*To our children*

# Contents

# Figures

# Introduction

This book builds on the legacy of work by Hobbs and May (1993) and Bell and Newby (1977), some of the first researchers to publish collections of personal accounts of doing social research. Telling stories is a natural part of the human condition (Barthes 1977). They help us to understand our worlds, enable us to explore who we are and facilitate our interactions with others. Indeed, such is the inevitability of narratives it is argued to be problematical only in a culture in which they are absent (White 1980:5). Here, in this book, we tell some of our stories with the aim of shining a light on the ways in which research with children is constructed, conducted and critiqued. Moving from the proscriptive accounts of how research should be conducted, the latter decades of the 20th century saw a rise in the explicit consideration of research as far from straightforward (see, for example, Devine and Heath 1999). This book emphasises that by acknowledging and talking about these challenges and ethical dilemmas, students, academics, researchers and practitioners are better placed to engage in empirical research with children.

The rise in telling stories across the social sciences to understand the landscapes of our world (See Frank 2010; Oakley 2007; Plummer 2001) developed in parallel with an increased interest in the stories of children and childhood (Cockburn 1998; James and Prout 1997; Wall 2010). Telling stories is not new, exploring ethics in the research process is not new and, as shall be seen in Chapter 1, research with children certainly is not new either. In fact, research with children is now well enough established to withstand reflexive critique that is aimed at strengthening rather than diminishing the field (Gallacher and Gallagher 2008). This book is a collection of stories that don't often get told: the messiness, the ambiguities and the parts of our research that lay on the cutting room floor. A desire to present sanitised versions that document research means the presentation of any narrative which focuses on the emotions or problems of research is tainted with anxiety and as such the public availability of these stories are limited (with notable exceptions such as Montgomery 2007). The presentation of our stories does not mean that we do not feel this anxiety too. However, we believe the methodologies that promote participatory research with children are strong enough to bear this critically reflexive gaze. Research with children is mature enough to have developed its own 'cherished conceits, stubborn evasions [and] persistent illusions' (Segal 1999:118), produced in part by the canonical narratives of these participatory methods, which are often advocated as 'best practice', and too often go uninterrogated. We borrow Segal's argument by suggesting that these stories are what we 'need to study not seek to evade' (ibid.). This is our attempt to shine a light in some of the dark places of research to advance methodological conversations.

Traditionally, the voices of children, most especially young children or those who are verbally less articulate, have largely been silent within research. It is not that research has ignored children (because there is much literature that documents childhood itself), it is simply that children in Western societies have been traditionally viewed as objects of concern rather than persons with voice (Prout and Hallett 2003). Until relatively recently, they have tended to be placed within discrete sub-disciplinary boundaries such as the 'sociology of the family' or the 'sociology of education'. Indeed, the dominant research approach has viewed childhood from adultist perspectives on grand scales whereby performance or behaviour has been measured by standardised tests. However, since the 1970s, there has been a growing sociological interest in children and childhood as distinct social categories with a contribution to make beyond how we measure their development and educational attainment. The view that children and young people should be viewed as 'agents' or 'social actors' has to some extent alleviated their role as objects to be studied, emphasising that including their views and experiences could provide important insights into the nature of childhood. This shift in perspective fuelled a policy focus on children, and subsequently the 1989 United Conventions on the Rights of the Child (UNCRC) was formed. The increasing enthusiasm for the concept and practice of 'child voice' is outlined within Article 12 of the UNCRC and states that children not only have the right to articulate their opinions with regard to issues that affect them but also have a right to have these opinions heard. Additionally, Article 13 declares that a child has the right to seek, receive and impart information and ideas of all kinds. Following on from this, a raft of policies including the Children Act 1989 and 2004; Children (Scotland) Act 1995; Children (Northern Ireland) Order 1995; Every Child Matters (Department for Education and Skills) 2003 were introduced in the United Kingdom, and while they were designed primarily to assert and protect the interests and rights of children, they ostensibly promoted child voice by implying that children should be encouraged to contribute to decisions that affect them. Rather than traditional research methods of 'looking down' on childhood, the micro-level analysis of children's lives stimulated by the alternative rights approach advocates 'looking up' at childhood in a more contextualised way. As a result, there is now more recognition of their social agency and active participation, and such an approach has reached a point in its development where it can sustain critical review. These assumptions, just like those surrounding child development and unidirectional maturation that previously dominated childhood studies, need themselves to be interrogated. Such assumptions are themselves productive, shaping how we view children and how we conduct research. Our stories here question the extent to which these concepts are effectively applied and understood in the context of children's lives and everyday experiences.

There are many standard ethical considerations associated with researching with children and quite rightly so. The combination of concerns about children's capacity to understand what the research entails giving informed consent; conflicts between parents and children; and the avoidance of possible coercion by researchers, peers or parents to participate in research produces something of an ethical maze. It also creates tensions between researchers who seek to empower children to participate and hear their opinions and those who seek to regulate studies to protect children and their right to privacy. While sensitive to the implications of rights to privacy, we want children to remain active participants in research and therefore advocate an approach that regards the two as complimentary rather than oppositional.

Along with agency and participation however, often comes the over-bureaucratisation of processes and, consequentially, the privileging of voice. While the drive to hear and understand voices and the assumptions of truth opens up innovative practices of collecting authentic, spontaneous and realistic voices, it does little to engage with the epistemological and methodological limits of voice. The collection of chapters that follows presents a series of interpretive transgressions that result from our need to complicate notions of research with children. We were driven to gain a nuanced understanding of how these voices and experiences were sought. Indeed, as researchers, we refused to follow the 'too easy' ethical pathway and curiously examined the power relations that produce voices. In doing so, we raise even more pertinent questions such as what constitutes voice, who is allowed to speak and what does it mean to be classified as agentic? Why do we listen to some voices and not others? How do we listen? And what journey does the voice take from utterance to publication? And what are the ethical implications of these questions? We do not admit to having all or any of the answers, just an insatiable curiosity. Therefore, the stories embedded within this text are products of our practice of scholarship which created ethical narratives generated by real research dilemmas we wrestled with in the field. It is our narratives, which usually remain unexposed by formalities of research, that we believe play pivotal roles in our understandings of research with children and the construction of knowledge.

Storytelling or narrative research has emerged as increasingly popular approach over the last 20 years (Andrews et al. 2008). Lawler (2008:27) contends that the analysis of narratives is 'embedded within a hermeneutic tradition' of enquiry and as such seeks to understand the ways in which people make sense of their lives. Stories are produced through reference to other stories and texts in a selective process which builds not only a story but a presentation of self. There are numerous ways in which the term 'narrative' can be understood and applied. Here we define it as being ordered 'representations' (Andrews et al. 2008:12) of knowledge, in this case about the ambiguities, dilemmas and revelations of doing research with children. Our application of narrative is to use our stories to reveal particular interpretations and highlight multiple 'layers of meaning' (Andrews et al. 2008:1) embedded in each story. Madison (1988:99–100) argues that such experiences are meaningful 'precisely' because they can be told. We take isolated stories about our individual research experiences and weave something bigger (Alvesson and Sköldberg 2009:129), a narrative which questions how we construct children in participatory research and the implications of this social positioning. We do not tell stories about how to conduct research with children as others have done (see, for example, Greig et al. 2013). Nor do we provide advice about selecting a methodology or method (see Lewis et al. 2004). This book is the one you reach for when you discover that the ethical guidelines that you have based your approach on fall short of helping you navigate the realities and complexities of working with children and their families in the settings where much research is conducted.

There are, of course, many interpretations of data and research experiences that are possible depending on the research aim and the researcher. Here we use reflexivity to move beyond primary interpretations which focus on the research topic or aim. Instead, we explore events in the field and what they can tell us about the practice of research with children and how the knowledge about children's experiences is constructed. Madison (2005) claims that reflexivity is underused in research, even where it is an important element such as in ethnography. Perhaps such reflexion is restricted to the researcher's journal. As Aull Davis (2008:7) contends, 'reflexivity in its "fullest form" becomes destructive of the process of doing such research'. Here we use it to provide a more transparent gaze on our own research experiences. Telling our stories enables us to achieve this.

The relationship between reflexivity and ethics is long-standing. Foucault (1972) presents ethics as the process undertaken by individuals as they reflect on and comply with or, indeed, resist the moral codes which inform and organise social institutions such as school and family. This 'public discourse of morality' (Zignon 2008 in Laidlaw 2014:31) is argued to be an unreflective condition of our 'everyday social life' (ibid.) which is, on occasions, destabilised by what Zignon refers to as 'ethical moments' when such an unreflective habitus becomes untenable. The act where consideration of moral codes has to take place is what Zignon (2008:260) refers to as 'ethics'. Reflecting on the moral codes that guide and shape research is thus an ethical endeavour. Here we use this reflexivity to interrogate the narratives and moral codes, such as formal ethics guidelines, that shape how, when, where and what research topics children participate in. The tendency in research with children is to err on the side of caution and to avoid so-called sensitive topics, to the extent that certain domains and research questions become taboo and thus risk becoming absent from research with children. Particular topics such as intercountry adoption, disability or sex are drawn upon within this book. We acknowledge that all are readily constructed as sensitive, even contentious, topics and considered even more so when it is children who are the intended research participants. These topics often serve to destabilise the moral order (Zignon 2008) as they cross the boundaries that adults have constructed around the normative themes of research with children. Constructing such significant boundaries around children and childhood within research risks contributing to the structural vulnerability of children and reproducing the discursive motif of the vulnerable child. Philosophical assumptions about the nature of children and childhood are intimately linked with the concept of innocence, equated with purity, irrationality and a state of unknowingness, all of which characterise the child as vulnerable (Kehily 2012). Indeed, as Robinson (2013) argues, childhood as emotional capital is infused with sentimentality, romanticism and nostalgia propped up by broad socio-cultural, legal and political practices, which are in turn reinforced by discourses of developmentalism. Transgressions from these cultural norms associated with childhood, particularly practices and activities which may be perceived to contravene childhood innocence, foster significant anxieties in society. These anxieties perpetuate stereotypes of childhood incompetence and myths and misconceptions about children's vulnerabilities. Thus research with children in so-called sensitive or controversial arenas risks transgressing the discursive boundaries of childhood innocence and is often considered to be ethically sensitive and, as the title of this book suggests, taboo.

Taboos are rules of behaviour which restrict the human uses of things and people, to avoid dirt and pollution and to manage 'matter out of place' (Douglas 1991:36). Taboos, Douglas argues, are held in the eye of the beholder and have little to do with real dangers; they are socially constructed and culturally specific but do function to label certain things and activities as right or appropriate and others as abhorrent (Douglas 1979). Taboos do, however, result in the formation of systems of classifications and social rules; the aim of this being to negate the potential disorder that breaking a taboo threatens. Applying the above ideas to childhood and research with children, certain topics are perceived as taboo, crossing some invisible yet powerful boundaries which have been constructed around children and childhood in part to protect the discursively constructed innocence of childhood itself.

Innocence is the discursive essence of childhood, and one of the strongest taboos in the contemporary world is the defilement of such innocence. Therefore, asking children to share their views on topics which are constructed as sensitive or outside the realms of childhood risks unsettling the discursively constructed dominant social order of childhood innocence and unknowingness. Such taboos and boundaries are powerful and shape the common-sense way in which we view the world. These barriers are not arbitrary, and they serve to support the structures that are located within and between. We thus argue that such constructions of childhood innocence and the resulting topical taboos serve to reinforce the adult/child power relations that structure contemporary Western societies, contributing to children's vulnerability and lack of voice. Such constructions shape what we know about the worlds of children because they can only answer the questions we are willing to ask.

What we argue throughout this book is that what exists in research with children is a hegemony of voice whereby particular positions and arguments privilege or marginalise both what is being said and by who. This applies not just to the children being asked to participate but also to those doing the questioning. Just as researchers are often attributed the position of 'expert' on a topic (Danieli and Woodhams 2005) by the very virtue of their status as questioner, the positions they simultaneously occupy as mother, woman and professional practitioner, to name but a few, can render them vulnerable. This vulnerability results in the potential of having our voices labelled as flawed because we reveal ourselves to not just (or at all) being experts but rather subjects who are part of the co-construction of knowledge. Moreover, we don't display the objectivity still often desired within social science research, having views which are shaped by more than just the label of researcher or by deeming to speak in ways that are at odds with dominant knowledge in our fields.

This hegemony of voice occurs within the diverse topics addressed throughout this book: what we are allowed to research, who we are allowed to speak to and then what it is that we are allowed to say. Just as specific topics have been regarded as taboo in research with children, certain conversations about the uncertainty and the messiness of such research are also perceived as risky. Thus, here we talk reflexively about institutional expectations, the spaces of research encounters, the voices that dominate and the topics deemed 'appropriate' to be explored with children. Within these pages, our hope is to promote a culture where, once ethics committees have been satisfied and when textbooks have been left on desks, the issues faced by researchers working with children can be interrogated and shared.

We have deliberately chosen to use our first names, as authors, within this book. This decision we believe is important in order to emphasise the critically reflexive nature of our stories and to avoid distancing ourselves from the conversations we're having with readers. To help readers navigate the content and discussions of this book, we have briefly detailed below the research from which many of the examples and themes are drawn.

Sarah's research explored the contested topic of intercountry adoption with families who live in England and have adopted daughters born in China. Data was collected through semi-structured interviews with nine families and one social worker specialising in this uncommon form of adoption. Nine mothers, three fathers and eleven daughters aged between five and twelve years took part in the interviews. Their narratives revealed complex belongings co-constructed and managed by children and their parents alike. It also highlighted the ways in which adoption discourse in general and intercountry adoption in particular is perceived and subsequently shapes the ways that these families construct their belonging. Sarah's research illustrated normative assumptions about childhood, such as their agency, vulnerability and dependence, commonly ascribed through the research process and instrumental in constructing roles considered appropriate for them to play. Identities which move beyond these ascribed categories are highlighted. Identity as fixed, autonomous and integral to a concept of self is revealed rather as being contingent, co-constructed and performed. (Some of the names in transcripts from Sarah's research have been changed for this publication.)

Allison researched with children and young people who have little or no speech and who regularly used high-tech Augmentative and Alternative Communication Systems (AACS) as part of their communication repertoire. The research focused primarily on voices – voices that are young and voices that are disabled. Specifically, she concentrated on the ways in which voices are simultaneously facilitated and inhibited. By including voices that are sometimes hard to hear, Allison's research built upon the moral perspective of respect for the role and status of children and aimed to promote their entitlement to being considered as persons of value and with rights. The participants gave their consent for their words and gestures to be used in this book, and Allison upheld their anonymity by using pseudonyms to replace their real names.

Jessica's research to date has focused on the discursive motifs of childhood, notably in relation to gender, sex, sexuality and sexualisation. Her work draws primarily from sociology and cultural studies to evaluate constructions of childhood in policy, political debate and media representations. Jessica has actively evaluated the dilemmas of researching with children in virtual worlds and the topics deemed appropriate for children to share their views upon. Her work questions the assumed vulnerability of children, considering children as interdependent and gendered beings who are competent in discussing, or indeed refusing to discuss, the landscapes of their own lives and experiences while simultaneously recognising how such worlds are structured by adult ideas and expectations.

## Chapter overview

Chapter 1 examines our experiences of seeking formal ethical review of research with children and young people. Rather than focusing on traditional conversations in this domain regarding whether research should be subject to such review and to what extent (see, for example, Dingwall 2008; Hammersley 2009), this chapter considers the implications for researchers of negotiating what can often be the contradictory demands of Research Ethics Committees (RECs). Here we argue that within childhood studies there can be found an ethical enthusiasm whose aim may ostensibly be to protect the well-being of children but whose actions, which seem increasingly focused on risk management, have detrimental emotional and practical costs for researchers and children and young people alike. Philosophical assumptions regarding the nature of childhood itself in the governance of research with children results in overzealous attempts to protect children and young people's welfare. This can result in the inappropriate inclusion of third parties in research and a lack of acknowledgement of children's competency to understand and thus consent to a variety of research endeavours. Taboos constructed around particular topics shape the conversations that children are allowed to participate in, and this leads to suspicion regarding the motives of researchers who dare to step beyond the normative boundaries of research. Such protectionism, as we argue, without critical reflexivity, contributes to the structural vulnerability of children and results in lacunae in knowledge where they, as participants, and we, as researchers, are unable to share our experiences and stories.

The places where such stories emerge are the basis for Chapter 2. Here we consider the implications of space, notably the home, the school and the virtual, for research encounters and experiences. Such places shape the data generated and present particular ethical dilemmas. These dilemmas are not absent in other spaces, but particular places where research with children is common can serve to magnify and bring to the forefront particular ethical issues and concerns that must be addressed. What is clear from our experiences of the spaces of research with children is that the discourses of power that flow through research encounters actively shape the relationships that develop and data that emerges. Ideas that adults are powerful and children are powerless are both exacerbated and dismantled in such spaces. The relationships between researcher, participants and others involved (such as parents or teachers) are more ambiguous than the expected, normative relationships between researchers and respondents. We thus had to manage multiple expectations and roles such as professional or guest alongside that of researcher. These intimate, institutional and political arenas should thus be conceptualised as producing ethical dilemmas such as those relating to confidentiality, informed consent, reciprocity or privacy. Our stories reveal the complexities of such social dynamics that require reflexive ethical consideration. These stories themselves inform us about how children navigate the social orders that structure the spaces we attribute to childhood.

The stories told in Chapter 3 consider ways in which researchers could be prepared to step beyond rigid guidelines and boundaries advocated within traditional research methods in order to reflect upon capturing the stories of marginalised populations. The discussions explore the adoption of a bespoke approach to gaining informed consent and, in doing so, highlight some of the realities of upholding children's rights of participation while including them in research. The discussions expose a number of real-life ethical issues experienced 'in the field' and explore how ethical processes can take on a more heuristic and realistic pathway, rather than following the tried and tested, step-by-step research guides that do not prepare researchers for the messiness, fluidity and diversity needed while researching with children and young people.

Chapter 4 critically examines some of the key concepts, such as agency, autonomy and active participation, which have characterised and dominated contemporary social research with children. The usefulness of such terms for the study of childhood are actively interrogated, questioning the efficacy of attributing ideas of agency or autonomy to children in order to understand their everyday experiences. These values emerged within Enlightenment thought and are characteristic of traditional models of citizenship, which are often argued to be based on an individualist and male approach to participation in public life. These dominant ideas of agency and autonomy construct an individualist rights position which is used to inform ethical frameworks such as regulations surrounding informed consent. These qualities are problematic because of the assumptions we make about the discursive construction of childhood itself, whereby children are not attributed the very attributes and skills that ethical research with children is premised upon. We question the appropriateness of these concepts and ask if alternative values might be more appropriate to reflect the roles of children as negotiated, relational and interdependent. We argue that rather than the individualist notions of agency, we should instead consider relational agency and interdependency as concepts which better reflect how children (and, indeed, adults) are socially embedded in the navigation of their worlds.

The aim of Chapter 5 is to acknowledge the presence of ourselves in our research and to explore the ways in which who we are shapes, what we find and why we find it. We use a specific focus on the

concept of category entitlement to illuminate the situated and connected category memberships of those involved in our research. Here
the purpose is to extend the debate that the researcher is influential, to go further by examining how this influence is established and
articulated. This chapter explores the processes of production and
interpretation of data through distinct concepts including category
membership, self-disclosure and insider status. These concepts are all
related to the co-construction of relations and the establishment of
authority to speak. Our stories here evaluate the connections created and negotiated within this research context and consider how
such relations build an entitlement for the researcher to ask and the
participant to respond. Particular membership of categories is often
the very reason for the participation of children in research, such
as pupil, young carer, unaccompanied asylum seeker, street child or
sibling. This membership has not only predicated inclusion within
research itself but also carries with it particular traits, characteristics
and behavioural expectations. These memberships are not necessarily the categories that children have established for themselves
but are commonly attributed to them. Nonetheless, we argue that
children use category entitlement as effectively as adults in their
relationships in order to make decisions about issues such as participation. We demonstrate here that their use of this 'tool' to affirm or
indeed resist such classifications enables them to successfully navigate research relationships. What is particularly pertinent are the
ethical implications that are brought to bear by acknowledgement
of these connections between the researcher and the researched.

Chapter 6 challenges the ways in which some children's voices are
privileged while others are overwritten by adults who talk at them,
about them and on their behalf. While acknowledging that including children with unconventional or quiet voices often presents
researchers with significant challenges and that facilitating their
inclusion requires a considerable investment in time resources and
the development of new skills, we use our research stories to argue
that it is unacceptable to exclude voices on the basis of incompetency
or because they pose challenges to traditional research methods. The
narratives contained within this chapter highlight the choices that
we, as researchers, make about the voices we listen to, how we listen to them and why we consider some to be more authentic than
others. Here we also examine how we use our own voices to share

our experiences. The ethical dilemmas associated with the dissemination of research are considered including the gatekeeping practices (Brooks et al. 2014) associated with both topics to be explored and ways of writing about and presenting data and ideas. Arguments surrounding the 'spiral of silence' (Noelle-Neuman 1984) suggest that ways of speaking are constrained by dominant discourses surrounding both research and childhood itself, and as such particular voices are rendered illegitimate and therefore silenced.

According to White (1980) narratives are only problematic by their absence, however we contend that stories about doing research with children are not absent but far less prevalent than accounts where children are claimed to be in some way active, empowered or agentic by virtue of a methodology, method or particular value stance of a researcher. Thus, we attempt to address the scarcity of such stories within this domain (with notable exceptions such as Montgomery 2007; Pole 2007; Punch 2002) by adding our stories to this slowly burgeoning field. The structure of this book aims to take you on a journey. We start in Chapter 1 where we explore how one might enter the field, as well as consider the regulation of access to particular voices, speaking in particular arenas. Chapters 2 to 5 focus upon experiences on the ground, where we tell stories of the co-construction of data and research relations. Our final chapter then considers what happens to these voices when we attempt to share them, how and where they can be heard and who listens. Throughout, we attempt to reflect upon the moral orders of research with children, questioning some of the persistent illusions and cherished conceits (Segal 1999) of the institution of childhood itself. We argue that such interrogation is what the practice of 'doing ethics' is all about and that these stories are what we should engage with rather than evade. This book then has become our ethical moment.

# 1
# Boundaries and Battlegrounds: Negotiating Formal Ethical Approval for Research with Children and Young People

The Nuremberg Code (1947) and the Declaration of Helsinki (1964) are both heralded as the result of what are now widely recognised as notorious examples of unethical research including the Tuskegee syphilis study from the 1930s to the 1970s and Stanley Milgram's obedience research in the 1960s, not to mention the atrocities that took place during the Holocaust. These formal protocols and frameworks, developed in the United States and Western Europe, aim to guide the ethical conduct of human research and have seeped from governing medical research into other disciplines including the social sciences. These trends have led to the establishment of Research Ethics Committees (RECs) (known internationally by different terms: for example, Institutional Review Boards (IRBs) in North America) in a range of institutions including the United Kingdom's National Health Service, research councils such as the Economic and Social Research Council (ESRC) and universities and Higher Education Institutions (HEIs) around the world.

The aim of RECs is broadly to guide and support sound ethical research practices and to safeguard participants and researchers alike. Both the committees themselves and the guidelines that they may make use of (for example, the ESRC Framework for Research Ethics 2012, British Educational Research Association (BERA) Ethical Guidelines 2011 or British Sociological Association (BSA) Statement of Ethical Practice 2002) have been criticised across a range of areas including becoming increasingly bureaucratised, drawing upon a medical model that is inappropriate for the social sciences and restricting potentially 'risky' research which is viewed as important and legitimate – for example, research on so-called sensitive topics or with participant groups who are perceived as vulnerable (see arguments, for example, in Dingwall 2008, 2011; Hammersley 2009; Hammersley and Traianou 2011). The discussions here are purposefully focused on the governance of ethical research in the United Kingdom as this is the context where our research has been conducted. However, there is a need to examine the development of ethical regulation more broadly across the globe, outside of dominant Western perspectives which run the risk of being imposed on a range of cultures in somewhat imperialist terms (Benatar 2002).

The aim of this chapter is not to engage in overarching arguments surrounding the degree to which social science research with (or, indeed, without) children should be subject to ethical regulation or the form that this should take. Rather, here we will consider how individual researchers negotiate existing formal ethical procedures and the impact of this on all the individuals involved. We will focus on three specific issues that we ourselves have experienced during ethical approval processes and that are growing to be increasingly common sights in the literature (see, for example, Monaghan et al. 2012; Skelton 2008): first, the positioning of children as providing assent rather than consent in the research process; second, the often imposed existence of third parties within research interactions; and finally, the governance of the kinds of individuals 'allowed' to do research with children and the topics that are and are not acceptable to talk about. Sikes and Piper (2010) highlight the importance of listening to researcher's stories. Narratives of such processes shine an important light on the often contradictory priorities of childhood researchers and on the RECs and ethical guidelines which govern their endeavours. We will explicitly consider our experiences of making applications to RECs for our own research and as dissertation supervisors supporting students in their first forays into primary research. In exploring these narratives, we will argue that fundamental philosophical assumptions about the nature of childhood and the competencies of children position children and young people as a homogenously 'vulnerable' group with certain 'sensitive' topics constructed as perpetually 'inappropriate'. We also draw attention to the emotional costs to researchers and supervisors of engaging with risk-averse RECs and the impact on the creation of knowledge in particular arenas, which are constructed as taboo and 'out of bounds'. Such positions foreground an overly enthusiastic principle of protection over and above that of participation whereby we risk denying the right of people to participate in research through 'unnecessarily protective and paternalistic measures' (Huxley et al. 2005:59).

## Children's assent versus informed consent

Informed consent is closely associated with the ethical principles of ensuring respect for persons (Brooks et al. 2014). This includes broadly three key principles: first, that adequate knowledge is provided to prospective participants; second, that consent is voluntary at the outset and throughout the research process; and third, that such decisions are made by competent individuals choosing freely (Brooks et al. 2014). This model of consent has been critiqued by particular scholars for being based on a neo-liberal, individualist and masculine model of personhood (Hammersley and Traianou 2012). It is further complicated when considering the philosophical positioning of children in contemporary Western societies as vulnerable, dependent and irrational (Archard 2004). Such discursive constructions of childhood have historically made it very difficult for adults to consider children as capable of offering such consent. Recent changes in the positioning of children heralded by the new social studies of childhood (James et al. 1998) and the United Nations Convention on the Rights of the Child (UNCRC) mean that assumptions of children's inability to participate meaningfully in decision making have been questioned. What concerns around informed consent reveal is a focus on the way in which power relations play out in research relationships (Thorne 1980) and, as is increasingly being considered in contemporary research contexts, the desire of institutions that govern research to protect themselves from legal consequences arising from research (Edwards and Mauthner 2012). The experience detailed below briefly articulates what happened to one of our dissertation students in their negotiations with ethics committees whereby the issue of children providing informed consent was far from straightforward.

As members of academic teaching staff, we all regularly act as undergraduate dissertation supervisors, and recently, Jessica supervised a student, Rebecca, who was proposing to conduct research in a setting that was also governed by an additional regional REC external and separate to the university REC. In this section, we specifically consider Jessica's experiences of supervising this student as they engaged in a series of negotiations between these two RECs. Rebecca wished to explore children's perspectives on healthy eating, using informal focus groups and drawings with children aged 3–4 years old in an early years setting. Within our institution, Rebecca's research gained ethical approval on the basis that her participant-led, child-centred methodology and documentation were considered ethically sound by the university REC. Due to the location of the setting, Rebecca also had to apply for ethical approval with an additional REC external to the university. This REC, on considering the proposal, reached a conditional decision whereby a series of requirements had to be met in order for ethical approval to be granted. The first of these conditions was a change of wording throughout the proposal and all documentation. This change entailed a shift from referring to children's 'informed consent' to their 'assent'. We use this example to consider the contradictory dilemmas that using the terms 'assent' and 'consent' in research can create.

Assent is defined as the child's permission or affirmation of agreement to participate in research (Broome and Richards 1998) and is regarded by some researchers as a substitute for consent so that children do not consent in their own right but assent to their parent's consent (Powell and Smith 2010). Assent is not a legally mandated process (Twycross 2009), and, in addition to cases where parental consent may itself be inappropriate or harmful, we question whether the upholding of dignity, highlighted in many ethical guidelines (BERA 2011; BSA 2002; ESRC 2012) and in key human rights instruments (Bell 2008), can be maintained while positioning children's agreement as lesser than that of adults within the research process, with their views and desire to participate (or not) as having reduced value. This 'fails to accord them the same rights as adults in terms of what their consent means' (Skelton 2008:23). Examples of this can be found in other research stories; for example, Scott (2000) documents that there was a desire in their research to use a cash incentive with children completing their version of the British Household Panel Survey (BHPS) to mirror that which was provided to adults. They, as researchers, had an inherent desire to place the same value on children's contributions as that of adults. This ideological commit-ment was somewhat constrained by financial budgets which resulted in the young people being paid a sum, but that was less than that of their fellow adult participants.

This issue is an example of how social research is 'a compli-cated balancing between many opposing options and minefields' (Hallowell et al. 2005:142); it also highlights the continued ambiguity about children's voices and the problems that still remain in attempt-ing to empower children and young people in the research process. As Lukes (2005) argues, caution is particularly necessary in relation to the least visible, and therefore most potent forms of power and ethics is partly, in our view, about avoiding abusing power discrep-ancies between researchers and participants (Alderson and Morrow 2006). In considering the positioning of children as unable to provide full informed consent (see, in addition, discussions in Chapter 4), we were presented with a motif of children as irrational beings with-out the desired capacity to participate fully in social life. Drawing on Foucault's concept of the 'examination', ethics review processes can be seen as disciplinary strategies that combine techniques of an observing hierarchy and those of normalising judgements (Guta et al. 2013) functioning as a 'normalising gaze, a surveillance that makes it possible to qualify, to classify and to punish' (Foucault 1995:184). The classification of children as incapable subjects reinforces the per-petual 'othering' of children within the research process (Lahman 2008), and such practices contribute to the more general powerless-ness of children under an adult gaze. Frankel (2012) argues that a barrier to children's engagement in social and moral discourses has been and remains based on the extent to which children are seen as competent to engage with moral issues (see further discussions in Chapter 5 on children's autonomy). Philosophers such as Aristotle and Locke saw moral reasoning as linked to full 'adult' humans, with children viewed as on the journey to such desired capacity (see Archard 2004). These philosophies provided the backdrop for stage-based psychological theories regarding children's development which emphasise the development of children and their ability to attach moral meanings to their actions. The risk here is that chil-dren become objectified as passive social objects, conceptualised as lacking the rationality and reasoning to make social or moral deci-sions (Clark 2014). This includes the ability to process information about and consent to participating in social research. However, we argue that positions such as these, those that use the language of assent rather than consent, fail to recognise the extent to which even very young children engage in decision making, whereby morality is part of the everyday life of all human beings (see Mayall 2002; Short 1999).

It has been argued that this can be attributed to the fact that traditionally RECs have not been developed from a child-centred perspective (Skelton 2008), and many organisations still lack explicit guidelines for child-centred research (Hendrick 2000). The principles and regulations that guide REC decision making thus appear to exist in contradiction to many of the approaches and ontological assumptions used in contemporary research *with* children. As Boden et al. (2009) point out:

> Social science has a long and creditable history of praxis on ethical issues, both in terms of research conduct and consideration of how the resulting understandings may be deployed.

The development of such work is evident in some ethical guidelines, for example, the BSA (2002), which are the product of long traditions of scholarly work on ethics and power in research (see, for example, Hollway and Jefferson 2000; Mauthner et al. 2002; Silverman and Gubrium 1989). These guidelines attempt to be widely drawn and recognise the need for researchers to make rapid and pragmatic decisions in the field (Boden et al. 2009). They do not, however, always offer researchers a useful tool for guiding or supporting decision making. As Flewitt (2005) states, she found little practical support in ethical guidelines to support the translation of general principles into actioning the specific issues that arose in the course of her fieldwork. In addition, such guidelines often do not explicitly take into account the methodological and ethical issues that may arise in relation to research with children or the development and role of children's rights, both in the United Kingdom and globally, on such research philosophies and practices.

Research with children, as advocated by the 'new' social studies of childhood (James et al. 1998), views children and young people as agentic social actors who actively contribute to their social worlds and, as such, should be viewed as co-creators of knowledge within the research process. The United Nations Convention of the Rights of the Child (UNCRC 1989) Articles 13 states that children 'shall have the right to freedom of expression; this right shall include freedom to seek, receive and impart information and ideas of all kinds, regardless of frontiers'. However, in the case of Jessica's student, the position adopted by that of the additional REC whereby there was an explicit desire that the student used the language of assent rather than consent in her documentation and research proposal seemed to be in direct contradiction to the approaches to research with children articulated in literature on child-centred research practices, taught by supervisors, promoted by the university REC and believed in by the student researcher. As Boden et al. (2009:742) argue:

> [B]y categorising people as vulnerable and therefore unable to decide for themselves whether or not to participate in research, ethics committees are accreting to themselves these people's power of exercising voice.

## Third-party involvement

Another area of contention in published stories of research with children, and indeed in the experience of our undergraduate student negotiating the contradictory demands of two RECs, involved the role of third parties within the research process. This relates to both additional 'researchers' from within the setting or appointed to surveil the research being undertaken and the storage and handling of the resulting data. Rebecca's research proposal stated clearly the plan to use tape recordings of the children's conversations while they undertook a free drawing activity if they wished. These drawings could be kept by the child, given to the researcher or photocopied depending on the children's wishes. This, along with the issue of the tape recorder, was addressed in the information letter and consent documentation for the children, the parents and the gatekeepers but was also to be negotiated verbally and ongoing throughout the research. The student had carefully explained the secure, confidential and anonymous storage of the research data within her proposal. However, the additional REC stipulated that the data should not leave the setting and that other members of staff within the setting would be able to have access to the data, notably the manager who held the key to the locked cabinet within which it was to be stored. There was a fundamental difference here in perceptions of ownership of the 'data' between the university REC and the external REC. As both a supervisor and a researcher, Jessica considered the voices of these children to belong first and foremost to the children themselves and, upon gaining their permission, the data could be used by the researcher whose duty was to keep it confidential, anonymous and to represent such voices fairly and honestly. The university REC considered that it is the student researcher's duty for safe and confidential data storage and handling. In contradiction, the external REC appeared to indicate that the setting itself and the other staff within also had a claim to this data, to be able to access and view it and to be responsible for its safe storage. We were puzzled as to how the student was to work with her data if it was not able to leave the setting. We also considered that the manager of the setting and the other staff had no right to see the raw data where children and their views would certainly have been identifiable to staff who work with them and know them well. Jessica considered that this violated the claims to confidentiality and anonymity, which the student researcher had made to those participating in the research, in the proposal, information letters and consent forms (with notable exceptions for safeguarding issues). This is not an unusual occurrence in research which takes place in institutions of education and care for children whereby researchers have to grapple with varying demands regarding the confidentiality of data. As Barker and Weller (2003) articulate, it is not unusual for teachers to want to hear or see interview data considering they have a right to do so, given the setting of the research in their classroom or their role as a gatekeeper in the researcher's access to the child participants. The management of such pressurised situations is not easy (Masson 2000) as refusal to capitulate directly contradicts the mechanisms of surveillance that dominate such institutions (Barker and Weller 2003). This is particularly the case for student or new researchers engaging in their first forays into research with children. This is also particularly difficult if such researchers have an existing relationship with the setting as a volunteer or employee, for example.

As supervisors, we began to reflect here on the insistence and appropriateness of involving others in the research process. Monaghan et al. (2012) also document that their REC requested an independent third party should be in the room during their research when interviewing the children who had agreed to participate. In Monaghan et al. (2012) detail the experience of Maria O'Dwyer, one of the co-authors, who defended her research from the inclusion of additional adults. Maria's decision was based on the argument that the inclusion of multiple adults in interviews with children could in fact contribute to the creation of a more unethical situation where the children involved felt pressured and surrounded by a multitude of 'powerful' adults. The external REC, having considered the proposal, listed by name the other staff in the setting and wanted their role in the research clarified. Our student had made it clear that she was the principal and only researcher on the project. No others had been identified, and it was through separate investigation that the external REC identified other members of staff in the setting and made a series of assumptions about their involvement.

The implications of such stipulations by RECs may appear at first to be small or easily managed, but they relate to wider assumptions about the ownership of data and the voices of children. Concern was not articulated here by the external REC that the children's experiences, what they had chosen to share with the researcher of their own volition and about confidentiality. As adults in the lives of these children, the employees and leaders in the setting in which the research was undertaken were considered to have a right to see or, at the very least, be tasked with 'holding' the data. The implications of adult/child power relations in particular settings is considered in much more detail in Chapter 2; however, as with the previous assent/consent discussion, what this experience reveals is a fundamental questioning of children's voices as legitimate and owned by themselves. They are somehow undeserving of the same degree of confidentiality afforded to adults by virtue of philosophical attributes of childhood itself (discussed in the following section) which deem them to be irrational, incompetent and vulnerable.

## Ethical enthusiasm in childhood studies: Taboos and boundaries

Ethical enthusiasm has been noted in childhood studies (Hammersley 2009) where Graue and Walsh suggest that 'one should enter the field as though on one's knees...not merely an entry ploy but a posture that one maintains throughout the entire research' (1998:57). The existence of ethical guidelines and their deployment by RECs are of clear benefit in prohibiting some of the unethical practices seen previously in both medical and social research. We do not advocate here that research should not be assessed for its ethical integrity, but we do share the concerns of other prolific writers in this field (Hammersley 2009; Hammersley and Traianou 2011) that such regulation risks closing down both the topics explored and groups with which research can be conducted. As articulated previously, overprotection in ethical regulation contributes towards the structural vulnerability of children reiterating children's lack of power and status within societal structures (Lansdown 1994). We argue that true protection of children requires protection of their rights, including that of participation (see also Miller 2000; Powell and Smith 2010; Sandbaek 1999).

The argument put forward by Graue and Walsh (1998) above impacts not only on the positioning, value and rights of children within the research process but also has costs for researchers. The literature that does exist where others have shared their stories speaks to a mistrust of childhood researchers or indeed any researchers engaging in topics deemed problematic, suspicious or 'other' (see, for example, Goode 2010). Goode (2010) devotes a chapter in her book solely to the difficulties involved not only in gaining ethical approval to complete her research with self-defined 'minor attracted adults' but in the risks of such a project to her academic reputation. Similarly, Monaghan et al.'s (2012) account of Maria O'Dwyer's experiences seeking university REC's approval for a qualitative sociological study of childhood asthma draws upon Hochschild's (1983) discussions of emotional labour, with the aim of forewarning and forearming other social researchers entering this field; they in fact dub their account 'a cautionary tale' (2012:66). What is evident is that the ethical governance of research with children has real emotional costs for researchers who, like Goode (2010), are often left feeling vilified, uncertain and devalued in their endeavours (see also Chapter 6). Fraser et al. (2010) posit a relational approach to emotions whereby they emerge between subjects and between subjects and society. The consequence of this is that they play a part in the social construction of personhood and to feelings of belonging and legitimacy (Monaghan et al. 2012). Researchers are subject to demands of including third parties, questions about their competencies and characteristics, and find themselves stressfully caught between alternative and competing agendas of various RECs and institutions. Thus they run the risk of what Stanley and Wise (2010: 6.9) describe as 'crying in the dark'. The costs of such interactions, Monaghan et al. (2012) argue, emerge slowly and accumulate over time during multiple micro-interactions. The dramaturgical stress of such contradictory demands on emotionally expressive bodies (Freund 1990) has real material consequences for social actors. Emotions are central when dealing with competing demands not just between different RECs but also between individual REC requirements and individual's own ethical conscience. In this sense, researchers can be conceptualised, as Boden et al. (2009:243) argue drawing upon Foucault's work, as docile bodies 'self-regulating and self-disciplining their own actions against particular ideas of what is standard and good'. This risks a reduction in the researcher's imagination and individual's ability to engage in innovative and creative work as effort and energy are channelled in 'easier' directions, and research intentions are channelled to fit a particular set of norms manifest in the relevant bureaucratic apparatus (Boden and Epstein 2006).

Foucault's concept of governmentality is useful here in highlighting how 'capillary forms of power insert themselves into actions, attitudes and discourses' (Guta et al. 2013:302), promoting the desirable behaviour of researchers (engaging with particular groups about particular issues) through a myriad of institutional techniques. This perhaps highlights the divide that some scholars have pointed to – between procedural ethics and ethics in practice that run the risk of sapping our emotional energy (Collins 2004). Although we promote in all of our work increased conversations regarding what constitutes 'ethical' research more generally and specifically, that with children, the increasing discourse of 'risk' adopted by RECs under increasingly bureaucratic conditions does run the risk of stifling researchers keen to embark on exploring often under-researched aspects of children and young people's everyday lives.

We too have shared disappointing and emotional experiences, like that described by Goode (2010) and Monaghan et al. (2012), in seeking ethical approval for our own research. Sarah's research with children and families regarding intercountry adoption was subject to significant university ethical review. This process saw her REC application viewed at a number of levels in the institution as various groups labelled the area a 'sensitive one' in need of rigorous ethical evaluation. What appeared to be overlooked during this process was that 'being adopted' for these children was not a special topic or issue, or one that necessarily rendered them vulnerable, but rather an integrated and embedded part of their everyday life.

Allison's research proposal was greeted with what she describes as 'horror'. The title of her REC application included the words 'disabled' and 'children', both of which sent the members of the ethics committee into something akin to panic. It conspired that this particular school within the institution had never received a call to approve a proposal such as this before, as they were usually dealt within the school of medicine or health. Similar to Sarah, Allison's application was heavily scrutinised, and, as a consequence, the process of approval took 18 months to complete.

Jessica was actively discouraged by a variety of colleagues and superiors from engaging in online research with young people under a certain age boundary (which lay anywhere from 16 to 18 years of age). The reasoning for such recommended restrictions was to avoid having to grapple with legal issues of informed consent for participants and parents, problems with affirmation of identity in virtual spaces and concerns regarding the well-being of children in online spaces more generally (see Chapter 2 for further discussion). In planning to conduct research with girls online about their feminist beliefs and political activism, Jessica was additionally advised to consider the prospect of entering online spaces but not actually engaging in conversations with the girls themselves. This was considered by many a less 'risky' approach than attempting to contact the girls directly, whereby there was no guarantee of appropriate adult consent. Little consideration appeared to be given to the reiteration of unequal power relations between adults and children by an adult researcher lurking in online spaces created and owned by the girls themselves. Additionally, by the possibility of misinterpretation by an adult researcher of online content created, shared and reconfigured for a variety of purposes and with a multitude of intentions by these young people. In other arenas where Jessica has presented her work on sexualisation and childhood, she has been approached afterwards by fellow academics who have dubbed her brave for embarking on discussions of such controversial topics. In addition, Jessica's workshops for practitioners on considering the positive elements of young people's sexual lives were highlighted by attendees as the only offering they had yet to experience as part of their professional development which did not focus on unplanned pregnancies, sexually transmitted infections and sexual exploitation and wasn't that a brave approach to take. In fact, sex and sexuality is an area which is considered particularly difficult for researchers to engage in with children and young people and is somewhat emblematic of areas which remain under-researched for particular groups and where particular voices remain predominantly absent. The result has been a distinct lack of children and young people's voices in such debates around sexualities, sexual cultures and sexualisation (Clark 2013a) – with the notable exception of Renold's (2013) research with 10–12 year olds. As stated previously, this runs the risk of generating lacunae in fields of knowledge (Clark 2014).

The 'difficult' topics highlighted above are examples of topics considered 'sensitive' in all research but particularly so in research with children. The tendency in research with children is to err on the side of caution, to avoid so-called sensitive topics, to the extent that certain domains, certain research questions become taboo and thus risk becoming entirely absent. Particular topics such as adoption, disability or sex, some of those drawn upon within this book, are all readily constructed as sensitive topics and considered even more so when it is children who are the intended research participants.

Philosophical assumptions about the nature of children and childhood are intimately linked with the concept of innocence, equated with purity, irrationality and a state of unknowingness, all of which characterise the child as vulnerable (Kehily 2012). Indeed, as Robinson (2013) argues, childhood as emotional capital is infused with sentimentality, romanticism and nostalgia propped up by broad socio-cultural, legal and political practices, which are in turn reinforced by discourses of developmentalism. Transgressions from these cultural norms associated with childhood, particularly practices and activities, such as particular sensitive research topics, which may be perceived to contravene childhood innocence foster significant anxieties in society. The phrase 'sensitive topic' is, we argue, significantly overused and underevaluated, and rolled out to cover particular areas of research as if it were self-explanatory (Lee 1999). Sieber and Stanley

(1988) define sensitive topics as those which are socially sensitive and dependent on the individuals involved, the topic or the context of the investigation. The advantages of this definition, as Lee (1999) highlights, are that they point us to topics which might not ordinarily be sensitive, but which in particular contexts are. This is often the case in research with children whereby discursive constructions of childhood, manifest in structural regulations, render particular topics problematic. In Sarah's research she recognised adoption as being a stigmatised family formation (Fisher 2003); intercountry adoption perhaps even more so (Johnson 2012). Defined in this way, adoption becomes a culturally sensitive topic (Hydén 2008) and triggers notions of protection. Nevertheless, being adopted is a visible and lived reality for the children whose stories she wished to capture. So we are forced to ask for whom is this a sensitive topic, and what role do such assumptions play in preventing children talking about their lived experiences when they are termed 'sensitive'? It cannot be assumed that this topic is universally sensitive for all families and children involved in adoption. Perhaps, as argued above, sensitivity might more effectively be perceived as relational and context-specific (Hydén 2008).

Despite extensive literature and research examples which promote the empowerment of the role of children in the research process, there remain boundaries and taboos about topics which children must be protected from, even if the topic relates to their own life experience. The field of research with children remains populated with children's perceptions of friendship, education and normative kinship relations. Far less research exists on children's views of contentious or, indeed, topics simply defined as adult (Uprichard 2010). What is particularly dangerous about such classifications is that the designation of a topic as taboo or sensitive is often simply assumed and rarely interrogated, an unreflected moral order in the ways in which we research with children.

Sensitive topics can be found in the diverse work of Farberow (1963), drawing on psychoanalytic and anthropological research, who labels those topics which inspire feelings of awe or dread as sensitive or taboo. Extending upon these anthropological leanings, explorations of taboo by Douglas are defined, like dirt, as that which can be thought of as 'matter out of place' (1991:36). In its original

Polynesian manifestation (*tabu*) it refers to a ban or a prohibition (originally, a religious restriction), but it's entrance into European languages can be perhaps better thought of as

> a ban on touching or eating or speaking or seeing. Its breach will unleash dangers, while keeping the rules would amount to avoiding dangers and sickness.
>
> (Douglas 1979:75)

Taboos are thus rules of behaviour which restrict the human uses of things and people. As with dirt, taboo for Douglas is held in the eye of the beholder and has little to do with real dangers, to well-being for example. Nonetheless taboos do result in the formation of systems of classifications and social rules; for example, in this current discussion of ethics committee. The aim of such rules and classifications being to negate the potential disorder that breaking a taboo threatens. Douglas's (1991) anthropological exploration of global societies in relation to religion and the supernatural points to the dreaded effects (for example, famine, drought or epidemic) that are perceived to be the result of breach of taboos. Taboos thus become broken up and extended to form classes and rules, and, as part of this process, we come to label things and activities as right or appropriate and others as abhorrent (Douglas 1979). Applying the above ideas to childhood and research with children, it can be seen that certain topics, for example sex, are perceived as taboo, crossing some invisible yet powerful boundaries which have been constructed around children and childhood to protect the discursively constructed innocence of childhood itself. The potential implications of this for research with children are that particular groups perceived as 'vulnerable', particular situations or contexts thought of as 'inappropriate' and particular topics constructed as taboo or sensitive, risk becoming marginalised by both researchers and the groups and committees that govern research for the very risks to the social order that they pose.

In *Purity and Danger* (1991), extending on explorations of taboos, Douglas theorises that the difference between purity and impurity is a question, like that with taboo and dirt, of matter out of place. The classification of impure is applied to an object or subject, which transgresses the overarching social system. For example, the researcher, who dares to tread paths into exploring sensitive topics, or the child who is given the opportunity to speak about topics that we as adults find uncomfortable. As a result of human need for order, 'our pollution behaviour is the reaction which condemns any object or idea likely to confuse or contradict classifications' (1991:36). As Duchinksy highlights, purity and impurity are best thought of as 'an assessment of particular phenomena in terms of what is imputed as their relative self identity' (2013:66). That is to say, the further a particular phenomenon is from its socially constructed discursive essence, the more impure or taboo it can be considered to be. Drawing upon this discursive construction of the essential truth of an object or subject and classification of something as impure as evidence of distance from this truth allows us to explain the fear and anxiety that research with children often evokes. If innocence can be thought of as the imputed discursive essence of childhood then asking children to share their views of topics which are constructed as taboo or sensitive (by some as inappropriate) thus risks unsettling the discursively constructed dominant social order of childhood innocence and unknowingness.

If, indeed, we are to aspire to Foucault's concept of egarement – 'straying afield or distancing oneself from normative definitions of morality...to attempt to gain a critical, usefully knowledgeable perspective' (Boden et al. 2009:728), we need to challenge such boundaries of acceptability. To be ethical in Foucault's terms is thus to reflect upon such classifications of normative and taboo and, as a result, either to comply or to resist the moral order. However, crossing these boundaries leads us to dangerous territory. The experiences of academics such as Goode (2010) demonstrate that there can be both professional career and personal emotional costs to working in these contested landscapes (see also Channel 4 Press 2014). The experiences of a fellow academic, Ken Plummer, who was lambasted in the press for exploring at an academic conference the social construction of paedophilia are also indicative of this (Gilligan 2014). In the reporting, there was an expression of disgust that public money for social research would be spent, supporting such events which were so clearly outside of the normative moral order of accepted knowledge. The impact of this can be felt amongst bodies of knowledge as topics become sanitised, inhibited and censored. This impact is not just amongst the academics who may come to fear they cannot ask but also amongst particular groups who never get the chance to answer.

## Conclusion

The problems identified in this chapter coalesce to provide a picture of ethical approval in research with children as far from straightforward and, perhaps more pertinently, inherently contradictory. These contradictions exist in terms of what research can be undertaken with children, who has the authority to undertake such projects and how children are viewed within these processes. We have also highlighted that, despite calls for increased multi-disciplinary approaches to ethical regulation (Alderson and Morrow 2006), individual RECs often act at cross-purposes prioritising particular philosophies, discourses and bodies of knowledge. This in itself poses serious challenges for all researchers as they attempt to appease competing agendas. It runs the risk of closing down research with children, particularly for new or student researchers without the resources, time or power to negotiate such contradictions and to challenge associated decisions and decision-making processes. It can be argued that this accumulation of power by institutions and their management is the product of the rise of managerialism and declining trust in professionals (Boden et al. 2009) in the context of the risk society (Beck 1992; Giddens 1991a). It certainly seems this way when we consider the prominence of requests for third-party involvement in researcher's interaction with children and/or the research data, the positioning of children's consent as diminished in comparison to adults and the labelling of particular topics as sensitive and thus to some extent prohibited or at least marginalised. Our experiences with our own university REC have been far more positive than that described by Monaghan et al. (2012) or Skelton (2008); however, there are vast differences in the requirements and philosophies of such committees as the student experience, articulated above, demonstrates. This can create significant problems for even the most experienced of researchers as they attempt to please and appease competing agendas and pose a risk for new or student researchers by closing down research with children altogether where a middle ground between agendas and priorities is not easy to find.

By reflecting critically upon such research governance, it is possible to explicitly consider the wider philosophies, classifications and moral orders which underpin such decision making. Using Foucault's concept of the 'examination' to conceptualise ethical review processes allows us to see them as disciplinary strategies that combine techniques of an observing hierarchy and those of normalising judgements. It is a normalising gaze, a surveillance that makes it possible to qualify, to classify and to punish' (Foucault 1995:184). This examination can be situated within the wider framework of governance and governmentality whereby ethics review processes are conceptualised as strategies of power. The positioning of children as vulnerable subjects, incapable of providing full consent to take full ownership of their voices or to comment on particular areas of social life or their own experiences, reinforces the discursive power of the labels 'adult' and 'child' within wider society. Even if we take the position that children are perpetually othered within the research process as a result of inherent differences between 'adult' and 'child' (Lahman 2008), it is still possible to view the disciplinary processes that govern ethics review as contributing to the powerlessness of children and, indeed, researchers. When children are denied a voice about a significant aspect of their lives, they are denied the ability to represent themselves as they would want to be seen (Holland 1992). By relying on terms such as 'assent', insistence on often inappropriate third-party involvement and positioning certain topics as out of bounds, sensitive or taboo can be viewed as disciplinary strategies that reify children's subordinated and vulnerable status, creating research which may be considered as less 'risky' but is simultaneously potentially less 'ethical'.

# 2
# Ethical Spaces and Places

## Introduction

The discipline of children's geographies reached critical mass in the late 1990s (Holloway and Valentine 2000) with the dedicated *Children's Geographies* journal launching in 2003, now issued six times per year. This signalled an increasing interest by social scientists in the spaces and places of childhood and the role of space and place in children's lives. Given this interest, it is no surprise that children's geographers and other childhood researchers have, in recent years, begun to pay increasingly explicit attention to the role of space and place in the conducting of research with children (Barker and Weller 2003; Pole 2007; Wang 2012).

The concept of place is an abstract one, but this has been defined by both geographers and, more broadly, social scientists as a combination of 'physical place, understandings of place...and processes of place making' (Clark 2013b:273). Following the work of Pink (2012:24), place can be considered as 'actual experienced environments and the practices that form a part of these'. Given these definitions then it is imperative that the principles and practices of research with children should pay significant attention to the places and spaces within which such research is conducted as significantly influential on all aspects of the research process. This includes everything from the development of guidelines for ethical research with children as a product of specific cultural, geographical and temporal thinking (Abebe and Bessell 2014); the provision of information to potential participants (David et al. 2001); the identity and positionality of researchers in particular fields such as the child's bedroom (Pole 2007); the conditions under which informed consent is given freely or perhaps otherwise (Heath et al. 2007); and the gathering and dissemination of data (Corsaro 1997). This chapter aims to critically consider some of the ethical issues that we as researchers have encountered when planning and conducting research across particular spaces and places. Here we position research encounters as socially and spatially embedded, notably in the home, the educational institution and within virtual spaces. As Herz (1996) argues research is context-bound and the associated ethical minefields should be addressed in a situational way. We thus argue that different places pose a range of situated opportunities and challenges in research with children. These are often not (with some notable exceptions such as Young and Barrett 2001; Barker and Weller 2003) explicitly evaluated or subject to critical reflexivity for their impact on the participants, researchers or data as well as their interrelations with wider methodological and ethical principles of research with children.

## Research in the home

Ethical decisions are situated and contextualised (Simons and Usher 2002; see also Plummer 2001) and are taken in the moment (Wall 2010; Zignon 2008). As such Guillemin and Gillam (2004) have argued that research guidelines are insufficient in preparing researchers for the complexity of the field. In consequence, some such as Yee and Andrews (2006) (see also Jordan 2006) call for more reflexive debate and literature to explore the situatedness and complexity of these ethical encounters. In this section, we discuss some of the challenges we encountered when the research field is someone's home, and we as researchers are cast and required to perform at least two identity roles: guest and researcher. We use our research examples with adults and children to discuss issues related to the management of self; building a rapport in the field, and the ethics of reciprocity; and negotiating the social conventions through which interactions between researcher and respondents in their home are organised.

Children are situated in specific geographical places where the institution of childhood is socially organised and reproduced. As such many children can be argued to gravitate between two specific

worlds: home and school (Jenks 2005). It is in these places where children are assumed to belong and are often perceived as being out of
place when in other locations (ibid.). It is therefore unsurprising that
these places are the spaces where much of the research undertaken
with children occurs (Livingstone 2002; Zelizer 1985).

Idealised notions of the home underpin our social understanding
of this private space. It is perceived to offer respite from the tribu-
lations of the public sphere, and, in the face of evidence to the
contrary, the home continues to be socially constructed as a harmo-
nious idyll – a place of safety, security, love and support that we each
aspire to be part of (Allan and Crow 2001). This private space is inextricably linked to the belonging associated with being a member of
another equally idealised institution: the 'family' (McKie and Callan
2012). Long-standing research into both these institutions has highlighted that each can frequently mask complex social relations where
differentiated practice and unequal power relations, based on age,
gender, ability and income, exist (Crompton 2001). Such inequality and abuse of individuals in the home has, historically, been easy
to overlook in the face of the idealisations and assumptions about
the home and the family relations therein. As Aarsan and Aronsson
(2009:499) argue, 'families are political bodies', the home is thus a
political and politically contested arena.

Researching with children in environments familiar to them has
been part of the journey that research methods have taken in a
post-positivistic period (Guba and Lincoln 1994) where the rise of
qualitative methods which value the expertise and subjectivities of
children has emerged as being not only the most ethically appropriate, but also effective in highlighting aspects of children's lives
beyond the traditionally dominant subjects of education and development. The home as an assumed place of familiarity and security
for children has perhaps not surprisingly become a common location for this research. Environments which are assumed to be familiar
to children – nursery, home, school being typical examples – have
been argued to promote more effective participation as a result of
that familiarity (Harden et al. 2000; Lewis et al. 2004). Hill (2005; see
also Mayall 2000a) has argued that the informality of home is also
more conducive to children feeling in control. Such empowerment
is representative of a 'canonical narrative' (Bruner 2004) in contemporary research with children but perhaps is more representative of a

'persistent illusion' (Segal 1999:118) in many children's lived experiences. Power relations that shape children's lived realities are rarely that unambiguous, and it is these nuanced power relations within each home that is a pivotal and recurring theme of this discussion.

## The living room as a research field

Research in the home is not without dilemmas, both social and ethical, and has been described as a 'triangle of conventions and negotiations', where the researcher is also a guest and obliged to comply with particular social rules (Mayall 2000b:116; 2008). Yee and Andrews (2006) also emphasise this guest role and argue that this identity is inextricably linked to the ways that the researcher is perceived and the social conventions that the researcher follows. It therefore cannot be divorced from the knowledge constructed. As Jordan (2006:172) argues these challenges are not unique or particular to the home setting but can be amplified by the more 'intimate and private setting'. Where in the home the research takes place also brings with it dilemmas and constraints (Pole 2007).

In Sarah's research the interviews with parents mostly took place in living rooms or at kitchen tables with coffee and biscuits. Her preconceived ideas about the homes where interviews would take place occasionally became explicit. On one occasion, she googled the address for directions and found distant images of the rooftops of a large and impressive farmhouse. Sarah accordingly wore clothes that were perhaps more smart than usual and certainly less practical. In reality, the large farmhouse was in part derelict and under extensive renovation with only a few rooms habitable. Sarah's shoes sank into deep, winter mud as she approached the front door on a very cold February day. She shared coffee in the kitchen with her participant and a rather boisterous hen, and the interview itself took place in front of a small fire in an otherwise unheated building. The farm cat shared Sarah's space on the sofa and periodically climbed onto her lap for affection. Sarah's main concern throughout the interview was not to let the interviewee see that her teeth were constantly chattering, thinking that it might make the interviewee uncomfortable.

Some parents wished to be interviewed with their children at home but without their children being present. They set up a variety of diversions for their children. One mother set out toys on the patio and had invited a friend of her daughter's to play. Their play was observed by the two of us through French windows as the interview progressed. Throughout this time, the girls knocked on the windows with a variety of requests and came in for refreshments. The mother apologised and responded in various ways. Each time Sarah suggested that it was fine and thanked the mother once again for taking part. Such ongoing negotiation of her presence in this home was a significant feature in how the research was conducted. As Lull (1985) has argued, the presence of the researcher in a home with a small number of inhabitants can be highly conspicuous. Before the interview ended, the girls came back into the living room, and the final discussions were more clipped and less effusive with some responses from the mother portrayed by gesture more than verbal content. This also inhibited Sarah's enquiries as she followed the mother's lead and avoided any inference that would draw the attention of the children in the room. Researchers in the home can exert little control over who is there and what impact they may have, but requesting alternative arrangements is not straightforward as a researcher seeking to maintain good relations, or appropriate, as a guest where a balance must be struck between the two roles (Jordan 2006).

One mother put on a DVD at one end of the room as the interview took place at the other. Hushed voices were used so that the children would not hear. This level of volume was not discussed by the interviewee, but when she responded to the first question in this way Sarah did the same in the following interactions. This was so successful that on occasion the digital recorder picked up the DVD sound over the quiet conversation. Jordan (2006) argues that participants can determine the quality and the climate through which these interviews take place. On some occasions, young children in the house who were not respondents wanted to play with Sarah who found herself variously being a guest at a tea party, a patient in a game of doctors and nurses, required to cuddle a loved toy and admire a painting or two. On one occasion, a younger sibling sat on Sarah's lap throughout the interview with her elder sister. Interspersed with the conversations for the interview are long-detailed descriptions of favourite colours, television programmes, teachers at school and best friends from her respondent's younger sibling. Her mother tried to entice her away on a couple of occasions, but she refused each time. Asking her to leave was not possible or appropriate, but her presence made the desired conversations with Sarah's respondent much harder to achieve and record.

Sarah also had to respond to enquiries about her presence in homes which sounds simple enough but complimenting information that the parents of these young children may have said about her presence needed some careful consideration. Sarah took part in these unscheduled activities in the interests of maintaining good guest relations as well as good research relations. Jordan (2006) suggests that the relationship the researcher develops in the home environment is less conventional than other interviewer/interviewee relationships. First and foremost, Sarah was cast as a guest in these homes, and this ensured that Sarah performed that role even at the expense of her researcher role. Stepping out of the roles assigned to her, and into the one she wished to perform in a space that Jordan (2006:174) describes as 'families own "turf"', deserves consideration and is, according to Coffey (1999), underexplored.

## The management of our identities

Narratives which emerge from fieldwork are situated, contingent and performed based upon the category entitlements (see also Chapter 5) of those present and the particular identities that the narrators select to perform (Mishler 1986). As Lawler (2014) contends, identities can be understood as being produced through the stories we tell. We argue that the location where the narratives are told influences the identity performances and subsequent stories which emerge. Such cultural behaviour can be perceived as a performance which has a long-standing tradition in critical ethnography (see, for example, Conquergood 1991; Denzin 2003). Carlson (2004:73) claims that performance theory is premised upon the recognition that

> our lives are structured according to repeated and socially sanctioned modes of behaviour [which] raises the possibility that all human activity could potentially be considered as 'performance'.

The performance of a researcher identity as a mode of behaviour in the home has been identified as underexplored and complex to manage (Coffey 1999; Yee and Andrews 2006). Maintaining a social distance is a research skill that is arguably required to reduce the potential of contaminating data. Yet establishing a rapport with respondents in their homes are also necessary skills for successful research endeavours. They are also social skills where reciprocity, self-disclosure and the building of an identity through narrative conversation are culturally expected. Holmes (1997) claims a gendered element to this reciprocity arguing that female listeners are more likely to contribute in this way. Gilligan (1993) links the kinship work of maintaining relations to social constructions of femininity contending that the capacity to be autonomous is, for women, commonly linked with an emotional responsibility for, and attachment with, others. These emotional responsibilities are not suspended during the interview process but are inextricably linked to the need to establish and manage a rapport between researcher and interviewee.

Cerulo (1997) claims that subjective identity causes us to address two key questions: 'Who am I . . . and how should I act' (Alvesson et al. 2008:6). Researchers are required to perform or act an explicit identity role that is not always compliant with the position respondents put them in as a guest in their home. These competing identities within the intimacy of the home can make remaining at what many researchers regard as an appropriate research distance, challenging to negotiate. For example, respondents often asked questions about Sarah's own adoption experiences having shared theirs in the interviews. Oakley (1981) refers to these situations as, when 'questions are asked back'. Maintaining good and guest relations within a semi-structured interview made it awkward at times not to contribute stories upon request and risk damaging the rapport needed for effective data collection. Examples of such self-disclosures are provided in Chapter 5 on category entitlement in this volume. Sarah gained access to the field in part through her status as an adoptive mother. Withholding this aspect of her self is not something she necessarily felt empowered to do in certain interviews though what was revealed was always the minimum amount that relations as a good guest would allow. Coffey (1999) argues that diverse values and expectations will be used by participants during such interviews and perceiving the researcher as a guest is often a role that interviewees have difficulty relinquishing (Bird 2003). Sarah's interviews often lasted for a number of hours and she frequently found herself being invited for lunch or dinner. On three occasions the original arrangement included a meal at the insistence of the respondents. It was therefore constructed at the outset as a social occasion by these respondents.

Coffey (1999) and Luff (1999) both argue that participants can frequently be active in determining the nature of the interaction between the researcher and the researched. First and foremost Sarah was treated as a guest in these homes and this ensured that she performed that role even at the expense of her researcher role. This negotiation often used category entitlements (discussed in Chapter 5) and competing roles of researcher and guest which were hierarchically organised and dynamic within each interview relationship and social context.

Maintaining good relations is instrumental in the construction of the following narrative where a professional social worker talks to Sarah about people like Sarah. Intercountry adoption is uncommon in the UK in part due to professional anxieties concerning how children can acquire the necessary skills about managing racism from parents who have or are assumed to have little or no experience of it (see, for example, Barn and Kirton 2012). Other concerns which highlight how such adoptions are regulated and exploited internationally (see, for example, Smolin 2006), also ensure that these adoptions, though possible, are unusual in the UK. Treated as a private endeavour the financial costs of such adoptions are high and this cost is met by the applicants. This fosters a general assumption of wealth attached to those who adopt this way. Such topics are not easy to discuss when the researcher asking the questions is known to be an adopter and the person responding to these questions is a social worker. These dynamics are only further complicated by the conventions of being a guest. In this case, the interview was taking place in Sarah's home at the request of the interviewee.

In the following account, the social worker rather neatly turns the negative 'consumer' category frequently attributed to intercountry adopters into autonomous and neo-liberal aspirations that become seemingly complementary to those who engage in such adoption applications.

Anne: 'The commitment is huge, the effort is huge. People who are used to negotiating their lives who make decisions and have successful careers, they are also used to getting their own way and having a level of success. They are therefore more confident because that is their experience. If they work hard they get to where they want to be and undertaking ICA [intercountry adoption] is a mammoth operation. You wouldn't do it if you were a shy retiring individual. I suppose that they pay for the process and perhaps recognise that they are purchasing a service and are used to getting what they pay for. In my experience they are not as tentative about being assessed as domestic adopters can be. They are also less intimidated by the professionals in the process. That is not to say that confident people do not adopt domestically because they do. ICA's by and large are more confident about what they are doing and have done their research.'

The narrative above performs numerous roles. It uses the negative attributes commonly ascribed to intercountry adopters and yet manages not only to complement those involved but suggests that the adoption process actually requires these attributes (Richards 2013). Anne is aware that she is speaking to an intercountry adopter and this knowledge shapes what she says and how she says it. These narratives then are nuanced cultural performances (Denzin 2003). Anne's narrative constructed these identity traits as she sat at Sarah's kitchen table. The extent to which guest relations influenced Anne's narrative is not possible to determine without a further contribution from her. Jordan (2006:182) calls these influences 'tangible but immeasurable'. Rarely, if at all, have the attributes that Anne identified been regarded as beneficial qualities for potential adopters to display. More usually they form part of a critical consumer narrative about intercountry adopters who neglect the best interests of children in their pursuit of a child (Richards 2014).

Sarah's interviews with children took place in a variety of locations throughout their homes. On one occasion she was invited to use the table in a conservatory with a plastic roof. The draw and write activity began well enough but a very heavy rainstorm ensured that the digital recorder recorded the sound of heavy rain on the plastic roof for about 15 minutes, making the conversations almost inaudible. Putting the host in a position of finding an alternative space was not something Sarah felt able to do and so sections of this participant's conversations were lost to the rain and the maintenance good guest relations.

All the interviews with the children took place either within earshot or with parents remaining very close by in another room. Most parents suggested that they would remain out of sight but be available should they be needed. This is of course understandable with young children and a researcher that they are not familiar with however it did raise concerns about confidentiality that were never really resolved. In one interview, a mother remained in the room with her daughters when they did the draw and write activity, she made suggestions about what they might write in the various pages of the life book activity and prompted them about the information that they might verbally contribute. At times, she attempted to dominate their interviews. However, it became apparent that the elder girl (aged 12 years) was not acknowledging her mother's contributions or including them in her life book, despite her mother's growing frustration. What Sarah gradually became aware of was the performance of a rather typical mother–daughter relationship where power relations were being tried and tested with Sarah's research being one of the battlegrounds. The more the mother wanted her daughter to speak, the more her daughter refused (see Chapter 4 for further discussion), while filling other pages in the life book with her dreams, aspirations and friendships. In contemporary discourses surrounding children ways to articulate their voices are given paramount focus with little consideration of how their silences are used or what they might mean. The following section taken from Sarah's PhD thesis expands on this use of silence in family relations within the home (Richards 2013; Christensen and Prout 2002; Kellett et al. 2004).

## Silences as relational strategies

Haavind (2005:142) turns the contemporary notion of the child having the power to speak somewhat on its head by questioning the 'potential power for children in saying nothing' in situations where independent opinions on shared matters are not possible to enunciate. Her argument here is that silence becomes a strategy of participation. My data suggests it to be a strategy that some of the girls use in family relations and in a research context. In the following exchange, the younger sibling demands her elder sibling's compliance to the colour order of the crayons that she has devised and which they are using to complete their books with me.

Rosie: 'May, can you put them back in order please or then I have to sort them out again.'

May: [silence, no response or acknowledgment that she has heard]

Rosie: 'What colour did you just use?' [she shuffles the pens between them at this point]

May: 'Skin colour.'

Rosie: 'Skin colour and grey so that goes just there [places them back in her order] 'Black and red.' [then says] 'Remember to put them in order, red goes there remember?'

May: [silence but does not comply]

Rosie: 'Oh May I told you to put them in order, why do you have to keep doing that?'

May: [silence but smiles]

Rosie: [says in a raised voice] 'It's not funny.'

May: [silence]

Rosie: 'Put them back in order.'

May: [ignores sister but to me asks] 'Do I have to colour in all the skin colour now?'

I respond, 'No.'

May only uses two words to respond to her sister's remonstrations of the colour order in this exchange. Silence seems to be used as a powerful strategy developed in this sibling relationship. This silence is not about a non-response but is actually more indicative of a way of responding that neither agrees, legitimises nor exacerbates her sister's demands. However, the smile may indicate that she is aware that she is aggravating her sister (and not finding it too onerous to do so). I contend that silence here is a strategy tool that this sibling is using with good effect.

Current research with children promotes their empowerment to speak rather than a right to silence (Lewis 2010). It may have become more of an obligation and expectation than a right for children. There is recognition in the above exchange that silence is necessarily neither neutral nor empty of meaning and, therefore, that ethically informed interpretation of it should be reflexively included in analysis. Borland et al. (1998) argue that children are able to reveal or withhold aspects of themselves in context-specific situations, again revealing a limitation to the term 'participation' where children are concerned. Silence may be the compromise position assumed by some family members between being submissive and an open rejection which would potentially destabilise the family relations.

### Guest, researcher or teacher in the home?

Despite much research being conducted in the homes of children to enhance empowerment, informed consent and familiarity (Harden et al. 2000; Hill 2005; Lewis et al. 2004), we question the extent to which the role of researcher is dramatically different from that of a teacher in an educational setting. Waller and Bitou (2011) claim that current methods often used in participatory research with children induce pedagogical relations. Sarah's use of a draw-and-write activity was not intended to emulate school work, yet inevitably it did though this varied in each collection context. In one instance, the journal page said, 'This is a story about where I was born in China.' One participant read this, went to a bookshelf, looked up her birth province in the index of a tourist guide and copied out what was written about geographical location, proximity to the sea, population size and historical aspects to be seen if visiting. This was done in silent concentration and far more indicative of a set homework activity than the telling of a story (Figure 2.1).

Wim (aged 8 years), another participant in Sarah's research, confirmed her perception of the similarity between Sarah and a teacher throughout the interview by her continued compliance and deferral to her in decision making, and also through requests for guidance in spelling and for what I wanted her to write in order to address correctly the pages in the book. The expectation of being a compliant and good pupil often ascribed to girls is evoked in her transcript and her journal entries. Waller (2010:530) argues that school can embody and reproduce 'particular forms of masculinity and femininity'. Sarah writes 'I am uncomfortably aware that I selected a method in which this identity trait was profitable for me as a researcher even though my research took place in the children's homes' and supposedly was a place where they are argued to feel more in control.

As Sarah reflects on her approach in her thesis (Richards 2013:157)

A researcher's implicit or explicit use of power is to their advantage whether it is acknowledged or not, making such methods and this methodology less innovative and more reflective of previous approaches than some would hope. Jones (2001 cited in Gallacher and Gallagher 2008:505) argues that these methods

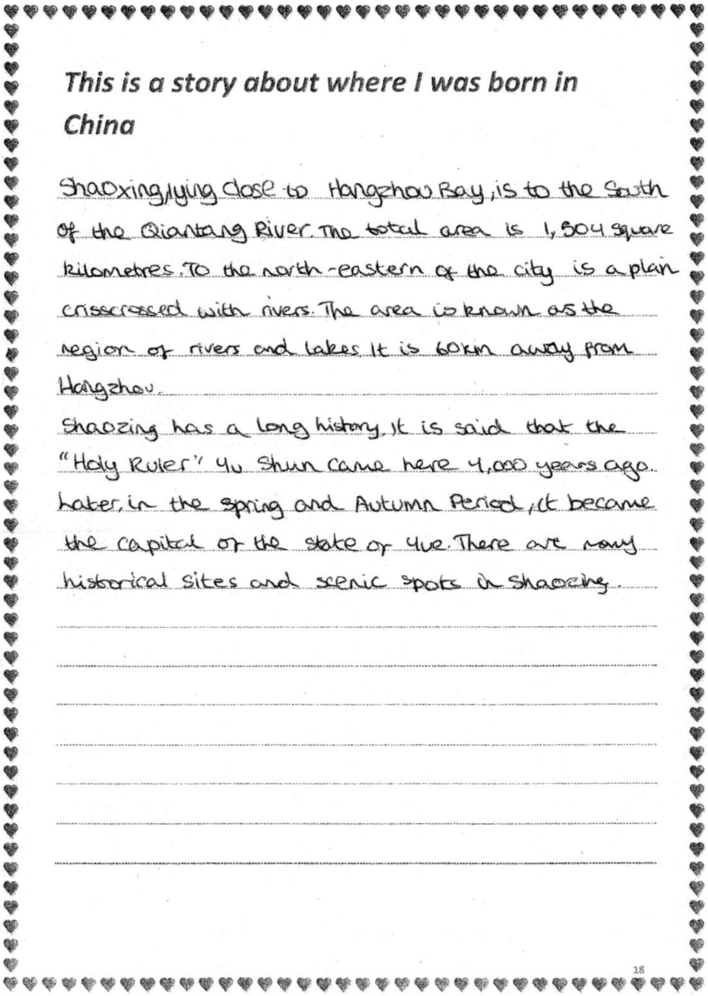

44

## This is a story about where I was born in China

Shaoxing, lying close to Hangzhou Bay, is to the South of the Qiantang River. The total area is 1,504 square kilometres. To the north-eastern of the city is a plain crisscrossed with rivers. The area is known as the region of rivers and lakes. It is 60km away from Hangzhou.

Shaoxing has a long history. It is said that the "Holy Ruler" Yu Shun came here 4,000 years ago. Later, in the spring and Autumn Period, it became the capital of the state of Yue. There are many historical sites and scenic spots in Shaoxing.

18

*Figure 2.1*　This is a story about where I was born in China

have less to do with emancipation of children's voices and are more representative of the 'colonization' of childhood by adults. However, I argue that the socially constructed space of childhood is already adult space and that this further incursion by adults represents a new way of exploring how children manage, negotiate or challenge the space that we have constructed and ascribed them.

I have reached an uncomfortable conclusion that, as a researcher I temporarily occupied the individual spaces of these girls, using a method which reflected their pupil role, justifying this incursion in part by the use of the language of inclusion and child centredness, and an assumed insider status as an adoptive mother. I also remain uncertain as to whether I have elevated the voices of those less able to speak about intercountry adoption in the spirit of ethnography, or participated in othering this group even further. The production of knowledge is not removed from notions of power (Foucault 1995), and it can be argued that for children to participate in knowledge construction about their lives is to 'encourage them to take part in the processes used to regulate them' (Gallacher and Gallagher 2008:504). Such tension concerning power cannot simply be resolved through the use of 'child centred' participatory methods where it is suggested that the children are actively involved rather than passively recipient.

## Educational institutions

Christensen and James (2001) argue that the spatial-temporal ordering of school shapes children's everyday experiences and Pike (2008) highlights the regulation of children in institutions through a range of socio-spatial strategies. Issues of power and control are central to an analysis of childhood space (Smith and Barker 2000), and educational institutions are key organisations where children's lives are constructed by adults and where children seek to carve out space and time of their own. School spaces thus should be critically considered not just as environments for children but as part of wider social structures where power is articulated and as places where meaning is negotiated (Clark 2013b). Critically considering issues of power and agency as articulated within and through the institutional spaces of childhood (the school, the early years setting, the children's centre) has resulted in a plethora of critical research which examines not just 'traditional' educational and institutional issues but all aspects of children's lives, including, for example, the role of different forms of childcare on shaping expectations of good parenting (McDowell et al. 2005) and the school dining room as a site of intervention regarding children's nutrition and well-being (Daniel and Gustafsson 2010).

This section of the chapter argues that the organisation of time and space and the distribution of power in educational institutions play an important and unavoidable role in research conducted within, through and about such spaces, discourses and cultures. Here we will consider the impact of institutional pressures on the provision of informed consent, the positions of power avowed to adults in such settings and children's negotiation of these assumptions and the role of gatekeepers in selecting, silencing and empowering children within such settings.

The issue of informed consent, discussed previously in Chapter 1, dominates discussions of all ethical research and is considered particularly important and complex in terms of research with children. The basis of the assumption of the importance of informed consent is one by which we should respect the autonomy of individual decisions to participate. The assumption here is that children have the competency to consent and that this conception of them as agentic beings is universal (see further discussions of assent and consent in Chapter 1). Aside from the fact that this model of consent is based on a neo-liberal individualist model whereby human nature is conceptualised as fundamentally Western and masculine (Hammersley and Traianou 2012), as discussed in the previous chapter, it is also clear that the ability to meaningfully participate in decision making is shaped by the environment in which information giving and consent seeking takes place.

It is well documented that children in institutional settings such as schools may feel pressure to consent to participate in research whether this is to be seen as cooperative by those in powerful positions, 'pleasing' a teacher or following school rules by being polite to visitors (Heath et al. 2007). Indeed, high response rates achieved in school-based research is argued by some to be rooted in this hidden pressure (Denscombe and Aubrook 1992). David et al. (2001) discuss the information sessions they provided to the young people who would potentially participate in their research. They chose whole-group sessions as the young people would be familiar with such ways of interacting as a result of their schooling experience, to adhere to their philosophies of assuming competence and as part of considering informed consent negotiations as ongoing (Alderson 1995). Despite this the position of the researchers within these information sessions was one of 'quasi-teacher' and as such like many researchers in schools they were able to make effective use of existing adult/child power relations. The spatial-temporal regulation of the school day itself allows for such whole group sessions to take place as children are ordered (by age rather than educational competence David et al. 2001) and adults in such spaces are positioned as authoritative knowers rather than genuine questioners (Graue and Walsh 1998). We all therefore as childhood researchers benefit from accessing such spaces where children and young people's lives are structured by existing power relations.

Such socio-spatial regulations do not always provide benefits to the researcher, particularly where they actively prohibit the voices that can be heard in general or indeed in specific spatial or temporal environments. Allison found in her research that a complex interplay of power operated within specific times and spaces within the school environment. She concluded that the young participant's voices were both controlled and restricted by adults. For example, she observed that during play time and lunchtime the children packed (or were helped to pack) their Augmentative and Alternative Communication Systems (AACS) away. While the children were strongly encouraged to use the AACS's in educational spaces such as the classroom, Allison discovered that school policies and health and safety regulations imposed formal restrictions on voices in social spaces such as the playground, the dinner hall or on the school bus. She also noted that during the day, some children's physical access to their AACS was restricted. For example, one participant's AACS was kept in a rucksack on the handlebars of her wheelchair. She could not access what she called 'her voice' without help and consequently had to rely on other forms of communication to make herself heard and understood. Indeed, the programming of many of the AACS's, completed by adults, focuses almost entirely on curriculum based language. Here we can see that adult perceptions of the need for children to communicate, to have a literal voice, are dominated by a focus on education and learning at a cost to the perceived importance of voices in the social spaces of school life. This can be seen elsewhere in research by Harden (2012) who documents the regulation of movement of children in a primary school classroom as entirely restricted by essential tasks for learning rather than for social interaction or emotional expression. In addition, Allison noted that the practicalities of setting up the AACS served to restrict its use:

> Sharon: 'Yeah, Justin should have it [the communication aid] with him all the time, but his chair is heavy enough anyway without the communication aid weighing it down...'
> Allison: 'It is quite big, isn't it? And does it take a lot of effort to get it on the tray?'
> Sharon: 'Yeah and they're not easy to use when the sun is shining, so you think, aghhhh, is it really worth the investment?'

This relates to Priestley's (1998:219–220) suggestion that the regularisation of socially structuring disabled children as dependent, vulnerable and passive has served to 'de-sensitize us from their agency as social actors'. Allison concluded that external structures of power such as those illustrated above regulate and restrict children and young people's voices and simultaneously highlight how oppression can be routinised in the daily denial of agency (Watson 2003). The justification of this as part of school policy or health and safety regulations demonstrates the power of such institutions over their members and in turn, their ability to participate meaningfully in all aspects of school life. Such restrictions have radical implications for the construction of data, the establishment and maintenance of research relationships, and crucially for the discussion here, for the giving of informed consent.

In another example from Allison's research (discussed in detail in Chapter 3), she actively aimed to respond to the differing needs of the range of children and young people who she sought to participate in her research. As such the ways she managed the giving of information and the negotiation of informed consent was not part of a whole group session that aimed to tap into wider commonly used and thus familiar pedagogical techniques but instead differed for each of the young people she approached. Despite childhood researchers advocating the importance of participatory methods and child-centred research to empower participants through all parts of the research process such approaches are by no means exempt from concerns regarding the potential problems associated with power and authority (Veale 2005 in Heath et al. 2007). Sarah's previous example earlier in this chapter regarding her 'write and draw' activity illustrates this well. Despite a research philosophy committed to listening to the voices of children and the provision of outlets by which such communication could take place the activity she designed did inadvertently replicate the kind of work children are expected to engage with at school. As such Sarah discussed some of the girls whom she researched with asking her questions regarding spelling, presentation, clarification on the tasks. In this sense these girls placed Sarah in the role of a 'quasi teacher' in the much the same way as the roles David et al. (2001) played in their whole group information sessions.

What the previous example demonstrates, alongside the manifestation of adult/child power relations in research interactions with children, is the fluidity of positionality and power. Despite concerns regarding the power of adults in educational institutions where social spatial regulations are constructed to rely upon, maintain and reinforce adult/child power relations what Sarah's example demonstrates is that children hold a great deal of power in these situations also, much of which goes unrecognised. As Barker and Smith (2001) highlight in an example from their research that despite what may seem to be the inevitability of adult power over children within such spaces this is not necessarily the case. When Barker decides not to play football with the boys as they are excluding girls from their activities 'some of the boys withdrew ... their consent for the research' (Barker and Smith 2001:144). In such spaces, it is important to recognise that children are the experts and engage in multiple performances as they negotiate what is required of them within such hierarchies of power. We enter as researchers occupy positions of power as adults but often lack the expertise of children, when significant proportions of their life are spent within such spaces, and they have developed and work to maintain in a diversity of ways. As Foucault (1998) argues, power is not fixed but slippery and exercised from innumerable points. The previous discussions of the potential influence of such spaces on the provision of informed consent highlight that power can be and is often structured in expected ways; that is, adult authority in schools. What is clear from the other examples presented is that power is more diffuse than simply this one-directional process; it is everywhere and can produce contradictory outcomes (Foucault 1998). Sarah sought to minimise unequal power differences between herself and the children she sought to research with but they positioned her as a powerful adult with answers to their questions. Indeed, when Sarah made it clear to one participant that she was in control, the girl in question simply laughed. With this simple act this participant made it clear that she was well aware of her position as a child and Sarah's as an adult and the implications of these positions for their interactions and relationship.

Despite the dominance of age based assumptions about children's competence research has documented that spaces of education and of care are interpreted and utilised by even very young children to manage power relations very effectively. Gallacher (2005) highlights how two–year-old children make active use of the spaces and adult imposed rules of a nursery setting in attempting to appropriate space and time for themselves. Her conceptualisation of the toddler room as a site of adult control for the ordering of children is entangled with recognition of the active role of toddlers as social beings in appropriating such spaces, highlighting the 'underlife' of the setting. What we must critically reflect upon here is our desire as childhood researchers to establish equality in our research relationships with children. In addition to questioning whether this is indeed possible given existing socio-spatial constructions of 'adult' and 'child', we should also ask whether this is desirable for children. Does positioning adult researchers as powerful actually make negotiating and managing research encounters easier for children? Researchers and the researched are positioned simultaneously in such spaces by a number of fields of power which intersect and overlap. Such spaces and the power relations that flow within them thus require critical evaluation to consider explicitly their multifaceted roles in the research process and production of data. This requires us not just to talk in accepted ways about the empowering of children but to consider the 'reality' of power relations embedded within particular spaces. Here we consider not just whether participatory methods can deliver all that they promise (Gallacher and Gallagher 2008) but also whether all that they promise is indeed all we should desire. Assumptions regarding what children want from a research encounter and what is 'best' for children to enable them to meaningfully participate regard equality as the ultimate achievement. This is not to say that inequality in research relationships is something to be desired but rather to encourage active consideration of how children actively manage such situations beyond simplistic declarations of 'agency' and our need to recognise this. Seeking to minimise power differences as influential for all participants within the research encounter may blind us to reflecting upon children's ability to use the fluidity of power to their own advantage.

Power within research in educational spaces does not just flow between the researcher and the researched. There are a variety of other individuals that are directly and indirectly involved within research which takes place within such institutions. These include a diverse range of parties including parents, relatives, head teachers, local governors and local education authorities all of whom play a part in the 'politics of access' (Barker and Weller 2003:213) – the decisions regarding whether researchers can work with children. Discussions in Chapter 3 illustrate Allison's experience of these complex chains of consent which somewhat ironically place children as the last group to be consulted as to their participation. In our experiences the role of gatekeepers plays a significant part in the negotiation of access to particular spaces, the exploration of particular topics and the participation of particular individuals and groups. Parnell and Patsarika (2011) in their discussion of children's participation in England's since cancelled Building Schools for the Future Programme are explicit in highlighting the role of adults in choosing those children deemed suitable to participate in the research and consultation thus mediating the range of voices which could be heard.

The need for gatekeepers is indicative of the institutionalisation of children and young people's lives (Qvortrup et al. 1994) whereby increasing amounts of children's time is spent in institutions for children and young people separate from the worlds of adults. Inadvertently, this often leads to children and young people not only being marginalised from the spaces of adulthood but their concerns and voices can be sidelined too (Heath et al. 2007). Gatekeepers hold the keys to give or withhold access to such institutions. This is not just a yes or no exercise but gatekeepers can also shape the direction of the research, the topics explored and the ways in which such explorations take place. For example, Dockett et al. (2009) explored family experiences of school transitions and one community partner withheld families with a history of violence on the grounds that the research would take place within the home. In addition, DePalma's (2010) explorations within primary schools of attitudes to lesbian, gay, bisexual, transgender (LGBT) individuals and groups was mediated in its use of videos due to concerns regarding parental reaction and their impact on school life beyond the research. In Allison's research, she clearly documents the positioning of particular participants by gatekeepers within the setting, including teaching and support staff, as able to (or, of course, not) contribute in meaningful ways to her research (for further discussions, see Chapter 6). She was told that Lizzie was 'difficult' and would probably not communicate with her. She was also told that she was likely to 'kick off' at any time. Here Allison was forced to negotiate maintaining a rapport with the adult gatekeepers in a setting while at the same time adhering to her beliefs in the value of all children and young people's voices. As with Sarah's discussion earlier in this chapter of rapport within the home and Jessica's explorations in Chapter 1 of an employee researching within their own workplace, maintaining relations in a group and/or setting that the researcher is familiar with within their personal and/or professional life and adhering to the philosophies of child-centred research is not an easy endeavour.

The role of gatekeepers although frequently problematised (as seen in conversations throughout this book), notably in relation to their role in gaining informed consent within institutions, also offer insight into worlds that researchers may be unfamiliar with. As Flewitt (2005) points out in her research, in an early years setting staff were able to offer a unique insight on occasions into the preferences of very young children. This did not necessarily entail speaking for such individuals by offering views on their likes or dislikes but in one example they were able to notify the researcher of signs in pre-verbal children of dissent thus potentially contributing to the management of consent with very young children which is certainly challenging. In addition in Jessica's explorations of the ethics of engaging with children and young people in research in online spaces discussed momentarily, those children and young people who create their own online spaces in the forms of blogs, forums and zines (see, for example, Harris 2003) are able to act as their own gatekeepers on behalf of themselves and their peers in negotiating researcher access to such spaces and the data contained within. This is something that is a potentially empowering experience although fraught with its own concerns regarding negotiating consent in the absence of 'corpo-real' confirmation of identity, age and adult/parental involvement: concerns which are not so problematic in educational spaces.

## Virtual worlds

Virtual worlds, as briefly highlighted at the end of the previous section, offer both exciting opportunities and new challenges for research with children and young people. In fact, online spaces, in what has been dubbed by some as 'information age' (Holloway and Valentine 2000), exist as a series of juxtapositions. While parents are encouraged to develop children's use of technology for the purposes of education and for later success in the labour market, they are also supposed to watch carefully and rigorously for the potential risks. Risks of children's engagement with online worlds vary from religious and political extremism to pornography to paedophilia and grooming and on to cyberbullying (Kitchin 2000). Such risks tend to dominate conversations about children's online social interactions, running the risk of being technologically determinist in their perspective (Bryson and de Castells 1994) where technology is divorced from a wider normative context of social practice.

Children can thus be viewed as simultaneously both technologically competent and at significant risk from these skills as they use them to interact online, which is commonly viewed as a public space (Valentine et al. 2000). Operationalised here are popular motifs of the Apollonian and Dionysian child which exist in parallel and have been identified as underpinning diverse policy orientations towards children (Stainton Rogers 2001). The Apollonian child is conceptualised as 'angelic, innocent and untainted by the world' (Jenks 1996:73) and can be seen here in the invocation of images of the vulnerable child at risk in the online, public sphere who must be protected so that such spaces can be used as effective learning tools. In contrast, the Dionysian child is considered to enter the world with a bias towards evil 'drawn to self-gratification and pleasure, lacking sensitivity and social control' (Murphy n.d.:6), prone to access inappropriate imagery or place themselves at risk by conversing with strangers and whose online behaviour should be surveilled or restricted in the name of protection, both for the child and for wider society. It is thus no surprise that it is therefore fears and problems with online spaces which tend to dominate conversations about how to conduct research in this arena: for example, how to assure informed consent (Kanuka and Anderson 2007) or the verification of identity (Pittenger 2003).

There is no doubt that children are increasingly using virtual worlds and technologies which allow access to such spaces as part of their everyday lives. Survey data suggests that half of all children aged 5 to 10 own their own laptop, more than 40% own a mobile phone and nearly all 7–16-year-old children access the internet readily within their own homes (Childwise 2013). These spaces thus become important landscapes within which to engage with children and young people about themselves and their lives. This section of the chapter draws on Jessica's experiences planning a project to engage with girls about their online political activism and the debates that such planning invoked. Here we will consider how online spaces can highlight discursive constructions of childhood itself (as with the innocence and evil discourses highlighted above) while simultaneously serving to unsettle traditional dichotomies of public/private spheres and adult/child relations. In addition, we will examine the ways in which virtual worlds offer both challenges and opportunities for the conduct of research with children and for the explicit consideration of ethics and ethical issues within such domains.

The internet has long been conceptualised by social scientists engaged in exploring the lives of girls (indeed, all children and young people) as having some emancipatory potential and for facilitating knowledge about how girls express their beliefs, engage in relationships and manage in complex ways their own embodiment and wider cultural trends and social change (see, for example, Aapola et al. 2005; Harris 2003; Ringrose and Barajas 2011). Jessica sought to expand upon these explorations in a project to examine the practice of feminist politics in online spaces by girls and young women. The aim being to explore how girls who self-identify as feminists use online spaces to present their identities, communicate their beliefs and practise their politics. Virtual ethnography was the planned adopted method for this project underpinned by methodological principles which draw upon both a range of feminist perspectives and the importance of listening to the voices of children. This was in response to methodological concerns that orthodox quantitative approaches dominate studies surrounding young people and politics (Bhavnani

1991), which don't necessarily allow girls and young women to articulate their own meanings surrounding feminist political participation and/or activism. At the very outset, this research posed a series of ethical dilemmas, most of which centred around the online spaces within which the project was to be undertaken. These dilemmas and the wider ethical considerations they inspired are discussed here.

Jessica's initial choices regarding how to engage with girls and young women, generating their own blogs and zines regarding their feminisms, centred on the use of virtual ethnography. This would involve the use of participant observation with conversations with participants to examine and interrogate the meanings they themselves attributed to their online content, politics and identities. This choice was a deliberate one in order to avoid accusations of 'lurking' (Richman 2007) in online spaces, which is viewed as akin to covert non-participant observation in face-to-face research. Lurking is widely conceptualised as entering virtual worlds and not declaring your presence, as a researcher or otherwise. There are assertions by some researchers (Smyres 1999) that these environments constitute public space and are, as such, fair game for the researcher, who can remain anonymous and silent. This is not an uncommon perspective and the issue of the dilemmas between public and private texts has been subject to wider discussion within the literature (see, for example, Madge 2007; Spriggs 2010). Some researchers take the view that such texts when freely available online are open to use by researchers without the seeking of consent as they are published resources which are publically available (Pittenger 2003). However, evidence from online communities suggested that some have expressed disdain at the invisible presence of researchers who lurk (Hudson and Bruckman 2004), and they have a duty to make their presence known. Indeed we argue that debate can become problematic when for example, researchers attempt to disseminate the results of such endeavours run up against reviewers who consider their use of such data as ethically unsound. It is not just the views of researchers and academics that differ in how they conceptualise such data but also young people themselves, with some research suggesting that young people view online 'stuff' as public (Stern 2004) and some as private (Spriggs 2010).

An interesting way to conceptualise these arguments is to consider whether we define online content as simply data to be harvested or whether we conflate such texts with the author themselves as a human subject (Bassett and O'Riordan 2002). This highlights an important point regarding not only the use of online spaces for identity construction but also the situatedness of online research with children and young people. For example, a young person's blog post, fashioned in a similar way to a newspaper article, might be considered to be 'text', but yet a social networking site such as a Facebook or Bebo page or an Instagram account could be constructed as an extension to the human subject. However researchers may choose to respond to such debates, what is key here is an acknowledgement of the potential, if we are not careful, to homogenise online spaces. As we have argued earlier in this chapter, the spaces within research are conducted is crucial for understanding research relationships and the co-construction of data – this is just as much the case with online spaces, not all of which are the same. Virtual spaces are a heterogeneous category where the virtual geography or architecture is just as important as in physical spaces when considering the construct of affective relations (Papcharissi 2009; Ringrose 2011).

We do not attempt to resolve what is now a long-running debate regarding public and private data online by offering answers here regarding what researchers venturing into online spaces should do. As Alleyne (2015:170) points out, in research endeavours it is researchers who must act as their own 'ethical monitors'. However, we do suggest that a 'free for all' (Madge 2007) in the virtual worlds of children and young people (and indeed adults) is potentially dangerous and ignores many of the debates that online research has the potential to inspire. Here, it is argued, we should pay attention to the cultural context of online communities and the potential for such spaces to inspire new ways of thinking about ethics. Madge (2007) proposes a hybrid relational model of ethics that incorporates text, space and bodies and involves a rethinking of procedural ethics which dominate contemporary institutional ethical review (as discussed in Chapter 1) destabilising established dichotomies of public/private, embodied/disembodied, writing/speech and online/offline. As Hine (2005) argues online research is marked as a special category in research ethics governance and thus requires new ways of thinking about what constitutes ethical enquiry.

After considering the fierce debates regarding the issue of public and private in online spaces, Jessica chose not to engage in practices

of 'lurking' as it was felt that there was a need to involve participants as fully as possible in the research itself, and lurking covertly
involved a level of deceit she was uncomfortable with. She considered
that the girls and young women owned the data they had themselves
created. In addition, as the internet as a series of spaces can still be
conceptualised as emerging, and experimented with by researchers
and children alike, assumptions regarding public availability remain
inherently ethically problematic for all. In addition, Jessica felt that
as an adult researcher she had the responsibility to declare her presence in the online spaces she entered and to seek permission and
informed consent from those who contributed to the architecture
of such worlds. As Livingstone (2006) argues, children deeply value
privacy and have made increasing use of online spaces to carve out
places and spaces of their own. They do this as a respite from otherwise increasingly restrained lives (Livingstone 2006) in order to feel
in control when much of their lives are subject to the surveillance of
an adult gaze. A fundamental reason for Jessica's decision related to
this issue of privacy was that she felt there was the potential, if she
did not make her presence known, to perpetuate adult/youth power
inequalities where girls' spaces are subject to an (invisible) adult gaze
(Smyres 1999). This position, however, posed different problems of
its own.

After making her decision not only to declare her presence in the
online worlds of the young people she sought to research with, but
also to engage them directly in conversations, Jessica found that ironically she was now going to encounter more ethical issues than had
she taken the alternative route. Not seeking informed consent to harvest publically available data seemed to pose a range of problems,
according to ethics documentation and senior colleagues. This was
despite a commitment, like fellow researchers, to maintain an ethical commitment to uncover the meanings of digital communication
as part of working with young people (Ringrose and Barajas 2011).
However, the desire to approach the girls themselves, to listen to
their stories and to understand the meaning they attributed to the
online worlds they had created, and contributed to, seemed to generate a range of issues relating to informed consent, parental consent
and age and identity verification. Jessica was guided on a number of
occasions to abandon the idea of speaking to the girls themselves and
instead revert to a form of content or discourse analysis, using only

the openly available online data. This guidance was premised on the thinking that her research would be easier or more straightforward if she in some way bypassed the ethical issues at hand rather than took the time to grapple with them. Such advice is not uncommon, particularly in the case of research with children, and anecdotal evidence suggests that inexperienced researchers and those seeking to work with children in new spaces (such as virtual landscapes) are frequently advised to avoid such endeavours. They are too complex, too time-consuming and too potentially problematic to warrant time and attention. What unfortunately is lost here is the potential for such research endeavours to enable us as researchers to reflexively engage with wider ethical issues and discursive constructs relating to research methodologies, online research in particular, or childhood itself.

The most problematic issue Jessica went on to encounter in the planning of this project was that of informed consent. This ethical principle is subject to much discussion and debate in methodological literature, as discussed extensively in Chapters 1 and 3, and remains so in virtual landscapes. Broadly, problems of identity confirmation are at the heart of informed consent being so problematic for online research. There is the potential that it is easier for participants to deceive the researcher, regarding, for example, their age, than is the case for offline research. However, this practice is rarely documented (Hewson et al. 2003). It does pose issues relating to gaining the informed consent of children and young people (for example, Stern 2004) and notably to gaining authentic parental consent, considered a must for research with children. Potential advice in this arena seems to be dominated by a need to affirm consent (Bruckman 2002) or indeed make contact with participants in offline domains first (Mann and Stewart 2000). This is a way of managing such issues and does address the tendency of some scholars to divorce online and offline worlds by not generating a binary between digital and face-to-face identities, worlds and interactions (Ringrose and Barajas 2011). It does, however, remove some of the advantages that the very nature of online research offers us; for example, the ability to access diverse populations and to overcome geographical barriers (Madge 2007). Such a model of informed consent, as already discussed in Chapter 1, remains based on a neo-liberal model of the rational, individual self, charged with minimising risk. Children are not comfortably assimilated into such a model when they are constructed within common tropes of vulnerable, irrational and dependent, and as such they are not viewed as competent beings capable of providing informed consent in offline or online spaces.

A desire to hear the voices of girls themselves rather than harvest data thus posed a significant problem. Perhaps some of the anxiety which children's use of and presence within online spaces invokes can be attributed to the role that such landscapes play in opening up the dynamics of traditional power relations between children and adults. Children and young people have previously been conceptualised as 'digital natives' (Prentsky 2001) as a result of their superior knowledge and understanding of information technologies (Livingstone 2006), with adults comparatively characterised as 'digital immigrants'. For the purposes of considering research with children and young people, such discursive constructions of children as knowledgeable, yet perpetually at risk, highlight how online spaces unsettle some of the traditional dichotomies and boundaries that dominate not only conversations about childhood but also research with children such as adult/child or online/offline or risk/opportunity. As Livingstone (2008) says, all activities are both risky and opportunitistic, and the reification of dichotomies of risk/opportunity is not a useful dynamic from which to consider children's participation in online worlds or the ethics of engaging with them in research within and about such landscapes. As Ringrose and Barajas (2011) highlight girls report being upset by pornographic material they encounter online (Livingstone and Haddon 2009) but also revise and negotiate porno discourses in complex ways thus affording new creative opportunities for sexual subjectivity online and discursive formations of femininity.

We offer no answers regarding how best to approach to gaining of informed consent online, the debates regarding public or private data or the other mechanics which exist regarding how to engage in ethical, virtual research with children. As Tapscott (1998) points out children and young people are relatively relaxed about the dangers of online activity and consider that adults overreact about such issues, the suggestion here is one of being sensible about risk and considering it as both relational and situated. While we have no definitive answers, we do suggest that an unsettling of boundaries is happening as more researchers engage in such endeavours. This relates not only to methodological issues pertinent to online research such as issues of privacy, ownership and consent but also to wider discourses informed by 'the virtual'. For example, binaries of adult predator and vulnerable child in conventional media risk frameworks (Byron 2008) and gendered binaries of female victim and male predator in sexualisation discourses (Duchinsky and Clark unpublished) can be unsettled if we continue to question what it means to engage ethically with children and young people online.

## Conclusion

This chapter has critically considered some of the ethical issues we as researchers have encountered when planning and conducting research across particular spaces and places. We have explicitly positioned research encounters as socially and spatially embedded, notably in the home, the educational institution and within virtual spaces. As Herz (1996) argues research is context-bound and the associated ethical minefields should be addressed in a situational way. We have thus argued that different places pose a range of situated opportunities and challenges in research with children. These are often not (with some notable exceptions such as Barker and Weller 2003; Young and Barrett 2001) explicitly evaluated or subject to critical reflexivity for their impact on the participants, researchers or data as well as their interrelations with wider methodological and ethical principles of research with children.

The home, the school and the virtual all pose ethical dilemmas to researchers who enter such territories often unaware of the power dynamics embedded within each social context and which shape the social relations that ensue. In the home, researchers must manage expectations of what it means to be a good guest versus a good 'ethical' researcher. Similarly, professionals and non-professionals alike have to manage power dynamics associated with ascribed roles in schools and educational institutions. Such dynamics shape the relationships which develop during the research process, the data that is generated and pose a range of unique ethical, situational dilemmas. Virtual spaces also offer a range of opportunities and challenges for considering the ethics of research with children. What we have suggested here is that such 'new' spaces, rather than being sites of risk and fear for children and researchers alike, actually have the potential to challenge some of the existing assumptions we make regarding children's competencies and about the governance of ethics more generally regarding, for example, the issues of privacy or the notion of a 'public' domain.

# 3
# The Rights of Participation and the Realities of Inclusion

## Introduction

As suggested in the introductory chapter, there has been a growth in academic literature that documents children's increasing inclusion in research and highlights their agency in terms of competency and knowledge (see, for example, Corsaro 1997; Haugen 2008; MacNaughton et al. 2007). Studies have also illustrated ways in which children are quite capable of making informed decisions about own lives: their medical treatment (Alderson and Montgomery 1996), living with terminal illness (Bluebond-Langner 1978), responding to their parent's divorce (Smart et al. 2001) and talking about their own experiences of disability (Stalker and Connors 2003). While much emphasis has been placed on children's rights of participation in research, we believe that there is little evidence that scrutinises the ways in which their inclusion becomes a reality. This chapter presents the reader with personal ethical stories that makes the messy business of inclusion and gaining informed consent more transparent.

In Chapter 1, we considered how researchers negotiate existing formal ethical procedures and pondered on the potential impact of this on the individuals involved. The discussions in this chapter will argue that while informed consent is an established and undisputed part of ethical research processes, it is a research term which is commonly adopted and understood, but rarely interrogated. Indeed, the paperwork proving that participants have been given appropriate information and a physical space to articulate written confirmation make up a significant proportion of ethics review documentation.

However, if we take meaningful informed consent to be more than just a name on a page, then as researchers our management of it offers us an opportunity to be reflexive in acknowledging the situatedness of research and the diversities of ourselves and our participants.

While researchers increasingly acknowledge children and young people as social actors and agents, there is a need to recognise divergent understandings of agency (see Chapter 4); for clearly, some children are attributed more agency than others. Indeed, Mayall's (2002:21) distinction between 'actor' and 'agency' can be used instructively here, with the former implying that children are of the social world (beings rather than becomings) and the latter taking 'action' forward, implying that children make a difference and that their views should be taken seriously. Agency should therefore be taken not simply to imply the liberation of children, but as an opportunity for opening up possibilities for hearing all children, consulting with them and creating new spaces for their voices. However, given the emphasis of articulation, rationality and strategy on agency, those who cannot give informed consent in conventional ways are generally excluded, and we believe that this negates their rights of participation. Arguably, research discussions that fail to incorporate a critical embodied and engendered account of agency in childhood studies serve only to reinstate a model in which conventional voices are privileged, prioritised and accorded more agency than those who have unconventional voices.

Tried and tested, step-by-step research guides suggest that prescribed methods produce findings, keep to tight schedules and meet standards of publications and accreditation. However, we found that this somewhat static, prescriptive approach did not allow for the modification, fluidity or diversity needed when researching with children and young people. Therefore, in an attempt to uphold children and young people's rights of participation, and suggest ways in which marginalised voices could be included in research, the discussions within this chapter advocate a more bespoke approach to gaining informed consent and acknowledge the use of conceptual tools sculpted and adapted from relational and specific practices.

The discussions in this chapter draw predominantly on Allison's research conversations with disabled children and young people who have little or no speech. The narratives recount personal stories of daily experiences of using high-tech Augmentative and Alternative Communication Systems (AACS), and the stories collected exposed a number of real-life ethical issues relating to disabled children's rights of participation, illustrating the reality of their inclusion in research. However, as a point to note, these conversations easily relate more broadly to the ways in which informed consent with children is negotiated per se. They also illustrate the often tokenistic paths taken towards the participation and inclusion of children in research.

While advocating what some might describe as a non-conventional approach to researching with disabled children and young people, it is important to emphasise here that traditional research methods have not been ignored. While it is true that dogmatic responses to research templates were sidestepped and intellectual common sense were applied to ethical guidelines, the processes used for seeking and gaining informed consent have not only retained credibility but become heuristic and realistic rather than procedural. By exposing and addressing these and other ethical dilemmas, the ways in which we, as researchers, can become more critical, considered and reflexive when seeking informed consent will, we hope, be informative.

## Rights of participation

It is necessary to critically examine the construction of disabled childhoods in order that a more nuanced understanding of the application and practice of their rights within research can be gained. However, childhood itself is a complex notion. There is never only one version of it, and this multivarious concept has been created through history and culture, interactions with others and by images of children and childhood. In addition, children tend to be united under one term: 'child', grouped together and unified, dismissing and disregarding their individuality and agency. The term 'disabled child' therefore not only describes and signifies the young person's developmental position within their life-course but also indicates the potential membership of a collective category (James and James 2004). Such collectivisation is problematic because assumed notions of dependency, incompetence and vulnerability embedded in conceptions of disability not only serve to shape disabled children's agency in general but also homogenise their childhoods. In terms of seeking and gaining informed consent from children and young people who have differing communication requirements, this homogenisation is not sufficient. The customary, standard written consent form not only excludes those with unconventional methods of communicating or understanding, it negates their rights of participation and marginalises their voices. Therefore, in order that universally accepted rights of participation apply to *all* children, processes that respect individual abilities should be used in order to seek and gain informed consent.

While acknowledging the complexities that surround the ways in which disabled childhoods are socially constructed, we also need to take into account the many definitions of rights afforded to children and childhood which draw on broad conventions such as the United Conventions on the Rights of the Child (UNCRC). Within this Convention, children are assigned a set of economic, social, cultural, civil and political rights spanning across three broad areas: provision, protection and participation. When challenging researchers to look more closely at the messy business of gaining informed consent, the reality of disabled children's participatory rights in terms of application must be critically examined, and it is important that particular attention is paid to one of UNICEF's core principles: respect for the views of the child. This principle is concerned with the rights of *all* children to participate, to have their views heard and respected.

Article 12 of the UNCRC clearly articulates children's rights to express their views, and promotes their capacity to participate in and influence decisions about their lives. In addition, the guidance and regulations dealing specifically with disabled children (Department of Health 1991) makes it clear that, if a child has complex needs, severe learning difficulties or communication difficulties, arrangements must be made to establish their views. While a disabled child should not be assumed to be incapable of sharing in decision making, it is argued that the caveat within the UNCRC (UN 1989) is potentially damaging to the general affordance of agency of disabled children: 'Parties shall assure to the child *who is capable of forming his or her own views* the right to express those views freely in all matters affecting the child, the views of the child being given *due weight in accordance with the age and maturity of the child*' (Article 12.1, emphasis added). It is not surprising that this caveat serves to negate the voices of disabled children and young people who are often assumed incapable of forming and expressing their own views.

We recognise that disabled children's rights *have* been upheld and they *have* participated in research and expressed their views (see Lewis 2001; Marchant and Crisp, 2001; Shakespeare 2006; Ytterhus 2012) but Allison found that gaining access to disabled, young research participants to be something of a complex, multi-tiered process. Indeed, adults created a protective 'fire-wall' that shielded the children and young people and while the young participant's views and experiences were considered central to the study, she found it curious that they could not be consulted until the latter stages of the process. Typically, gatekeepers and parents/carers' informed consent should be gained before the children themselves are approached. The protection of vulnerable participants takes precedence and subsequently the adult's voice is prioritised. This should not be surprising however, for the competence of disabled children to make decisions for themselves has long been debated within the context of research, medical care and in law. Indeed, while we should not forget that children's voices should be given due weight in accordance with the age and maturity of the child, we should remember that it is adults who ultimately decide whether the child is competent to make those decisions.

When challenging the application of children's rights and examining the realities of participation, we should also be mindful that some adults will not always support other adults who try to gain access to children's knowledge. It is as if they are fearful of in-balancing the *status quo*. Indeed, as mentioned previously, we should not forget that it is adults who ultimately hold the power to make final decisions in terms of allowing researchers to access children: what topics are deemed to suitable to ask children about and whether the children are competent to be included in research. While Allison was keen to find out about the lives of children and young people who used high tech augmentative and alternative communication aids on a regular basis, and the focus on the young participants as competent social agents was drawn from the discourse of the sociology of childhood, she found the data illustrated that mostly their agency was situated and constructed in terms of dependence and competency. Having concluded that the voices of disabled children and young people were inextricably interlinked with other voices and influenced by larger social structures, Allison began to consider the duality of the relationships between the structure of disabled childhoods and disabled children's agency as central to her work. She then turned to structuration theory to explore the interaction between human agency and social structure and in doing so, became intrigued by Giddens' interest in structuration in relation to 'the dynamic process whereby structures come into being' (1979:121) for he felt that anyone who was keen on establishing the origin of structures would also be interested in how they became structurised in the first place. Consequently, he set out to link temporal levels of analysis of day-to-day experiences with the relatively longer duration of invariant structures that stretch over longer periods of time. He suggested that structuration emphasises the processes of how human actors reproduce and transform social systems. He also believed that the more day to day experiences are repeated and engrained into daily routines, the more resistant they are to being manipulated or changed by individual agents. Similarly, the less they are repeated over shorter spaces of time, the less likely they are to be fixed in daily life and social structures. Allison's data offered a significant insight into the processes of the structuration of voice. Her observations relating to the nature and context of disabled children and young people's lives demonstrated how they contribute to social production and reproduction on a day-to-day basis. In accordance with this and central to Giddens' (1984) view of structuration, is the reflexivity of individuals as they contribute to social production and while disabled children's participation is represented by their lack of social status, Giddens argues that *all* agents can choose to use their knowledge and understanding of rules in a reflexive way to either conform or act otherwise. In these terms, it is important to consider that, within an environment that encourages participation, disabled children *can* contribute to the processes of childhood change. Indeed, as will be discussed in more depth later in this chapter, the disabled children and young people of this study as agents in focus, demonstrated that they had a fairly clear sense of their own power. At times, they felt empowered to speak out and at others, when they acknowledged an equivalent sense of the power of others within the same context, they chose to keep quiet. Giddens (1984) would argue that this understanding relates to the 'virtual' sense of power within relations which enabled the disabled children and young people to act knowledgeably. In a similar vein, Gilligan suggests that the choice to articulate or not is a contextual judgment and one which is 'bound to the particulars of time and place' (1993:58). However, while Giddens' arguments highlight the *possibility* of voice, Gilligan relates more to the *processes* of production and interpretation. It is at this point we should stop and reconsider the power imbalances at work here. While we argue that including disabled children's voices in research upholds their rights of participation and goes some way towards re-evaluating their status and position, if their voices are thwarted from the outset by those who are more powerful, the risk of their exclusion is very real. In a similar vein, Stones (2005:8) argues that analysis should be directed at the reality of particular social processes and events in particular times and places. While also emphasising the centrality of the duality of structure and agency, he calls for 'ontology in-situ' where human agents are viewed as being linked within dynamic networks of position practices. Indeed, disabled children and young people often find themselves within environments of pre-existing structures where social sanctions constrain agency and in terms of Allison's research, this indicates that while the nature of agency is fluid and contextual, actors' voices can also be shaped by pre-existing contexts.

It is important for researchers to build a realistic but critical understanding of such pre-existing contexts in the guise of the lengthy ethical processes involved when wishing to gain access to disabled children. Perhaps this, in itself offers an explanation as to why some disabled children and young people's participatory rights are thwarted and their voices are neither sought nor heard in research. Academic research journeys often begin by seeking ethics committee's approval (see Chapter 1). Generally, lengthy research proposals needed to be written, and ethical considerations defended. Once institutional approval has been gained, the consent of the gatekeepers (for example, schools) can then be sought. In Allison's case, the gatekeepers acted as intermediaries (see in addition Chapter 2) – sending the research information to the parents/carers on the researcher's behalf (because supplying prospective participants' contact details directly is not deemed to be ethical practice). The chain of access then became even more complicated and intricate: the school secretary forwarded introductory letters to teachers who passed them to the pupils to give to their parent/carers, who offered their consent (or not). The reverse system then operated when parents sent the consent forms back to the school via the children. Ironically, the voices that Allison was the most interested in (those of the disabled children and young people) were last in this complex chain of consent. Their participation, their voices and consequently their own stories were only to be heard once adults' agreement and consent had been negotiated. Sarah's research journey had a different but equally long chain which also involved parents actively shaping the data collection process (see Chapter 4). This is also mirrored in Jessica's experiences with concerns of not being able to guarantee traditional written and signed informed consent, including parental consent, in research encounters in virtual worlds. Jessica also found when supervising student research that the governance of research with children varies drastically in the importance it places on children's informed consent (see Chapter 1). All of these examples illustrate the challenges involved in retaining children's voices as foremost in research despite intentions to make them central.

## Seeking informed consent

As highlighted earlier, the introduction of legislation and international conventions designed to assert and protect the interests and rights of children (Children Act, 1989; Children (Scotland) Act, 1995; Children (Northern Ireland) Order, 1995; United Conventions on the Rights of the Child (United Nations 1989)) imply that as children are active participants of their lives, they have the right to be heard and to contribute to decisions that affect them. Article 13 (1) of the UN Convention of the Rights of the Child (United Nations 1989) outlines the child's rights to freedom of expression and the right to seek, receive and impart information. The implications of this for research with children is that it becomes beholden on the researchers to provide appropriate individualised information and mechanisms of consent beyond the usual and often tokenistic forms of written consent. This will also include recognising the diversity of ways in which children provide their consent or dissent, for example, through verbal and embodied indicators, as discussed in Chapter 1. In addition, Article 10 of the UK Human Rights Act (1998) incorporating provisions of the European Convention on Human Rights and Fundamental Freedoms (Council of Europe 1950) and applying both to adults and to children, is equally concerned with freedom of expression, echoing the importance of the rights expressed by the

United Conventions of the Rights of the Child (United Nations 1989) to receive and impart information and ideas without interference. Universal legislation and conventions recognise in principle that children are active participants and have the right to be heard and to contribute to decisions that affect them. However, tensions between the social processes of seeking consent stem from the continuing debate regarding whether or not children themselves are able to consent to participation in research, or whether the parents should consent on their behalf. The National Children's Bureau (2003) reflects the ambiguities of obtaining consent, believing on the one hand in the necessity of children consenting to participate while on the other, recognising the necessity of seeking parents or 'gatekeepers' permission to approach the child. A consequence of this is that if a child or young person consented to participate in the research but the parent refuses, researchers are obliged to respect the parent's decision (Butler and Williamson 1994). Indeed, as Allison discovered, if any of the gatekeepers – the school or the parents – refused consent and exercised their responsibility in this way it may, as Lloyd Smith and Tarr (2000) suggest, have impinged on the rights of the child to be heard, to express their views on matters of concern to them, be able to exercise choice and take action independently of adults. While it is beyond the remit of this chapter, further and more in-depth discussions of both the status afforded to children's informed consent and the ongoing negotiations that surround it can be found in Chapters 1 and 4.

## Realities of inclusion

Wright (2008) acknowledges the potential challenges of including disabled children and young people in research but argues that it is crucial that methods for fostering voices are sought. He contends that findings will justify research with pupils with multiple and complex needs as worthwhile, for not only will it provide authenticity, it will also empower those whose views and opinions are not usually heard. Indeed, researchers (for example, Badham 2004; Cavet and Sloper 2004; DeSchauwer et al. 2009; Morris 2003; Franklin and Sloper 2009; Watson et al. 1999) who have championed the need for disabled children's inclusion in research and actively promoted opportunities for their participation found that learning to listen and consult with young people provided supporting evidence which demonstrated that that they can hold and express views about their own lives in terms of their school, their families, the additional support they need and the services they access. As a point to note, Lewis and Porter (2004) produced a set of guidelines for critical self-evaluation for those actively engaged in systematically collecting the views of disabled children and young people, and others such as Stalker and Connors (2003) and Rabiee et al. (2005) discuss methods used in seeking disabled children's accounts of their everyday lives. Ward (1997) and Morris (1998) produced practical 'how to' guides in order that disabled children and young people could be more actively involved in research and development projects and Stalker (2012) went as far as to edit and publish a special issue of the peer-reviewed journal, Children and Society to increase awareness of disabled children and young people's views and experiences and their involvement in research, offering a range of ways of seek their opinions. While this positive inclusion of disabled children and young people's voices is to be applauded what should also be acknowledged is the complex relationship between voice, power and empowerment. Simply facilitating particular individuals or groups to speak does not necessarily change the power dynamics of their societal position or relations within the research process. Even when particular voices are heard it remains possible for researchers, in their purported positions as 'experts' to use such voices tokenistically or to engage in interpretation based on their own positions and understandings rather than those of their participants (Oliver 1992) (in addition see Chapter 6).

Cameron and Murphey (2006) warn researchers that they should consider ethical issues carefully when establishing whether or not participants can give consent to be involved in research in the first place. Their study with adults with learning disabilities illustrated that including specific adaptations enabled some participants with comprehension difficulties to understand the nature of their involvement and give their own consent but they also acknowledged that those whose comprehension was poorer presented researchers with specific challenges. Balancing the need to protect people assumed to be vulnerable from being coerced or including them without consent while simultaneously ensuring that they were not being excluded is clearly challenging, but in order to challenge objectification and silence, disabled children and young people need to be recognised as active participants and their input should be prioritised.

### Gaining informed consent

While earlier discussions outline the complexities of the process of seeking consent, in terms of recognising agency and respecting rights of participation, Mahon et al. (1996) believe that the process of gaining consent is of particular importance when researching with children and young people. Indeed, Kellet (2005) argues that it is not simply a question of informing the participants of the nature of the research and asking them to sign a consent form but suggests there is a need to carefully outline the aims of the research, explain how the data will be collected from them and how it will be used. Where complex debates relating to children's competencies, age and maturity, and credibility of their statements have effectively questioned whether their voices can be taken seriously, Rodgers (1999) argues that given the appropriate information and mechanisms, many disabled people *can* understand and make their own decisions. Acknowledging that many disabled children and young people require additional support in order to participate in research that seeks their views and experiences, Stalker (2012) upholds the need of flexibility and inclusivity within the research process and argues that a range of ways are needed to seek their opinions. Clearly, the 'one size fits all' approach to gaining informed consent is insufficient and including participants who have little or no speech requires improvisation and adaptation.

When researching with children and young people who used high-tech Augmented and Alternative Communications Systems (AACS), individual abilities were respected whereby Allison produced bespoke information for each prospective participant. Having sought advice from staff and an older pupil within the school (also a high-tech communication aid user), information sheets and letters seeking consent were produced that explained the research aims and the extent of their involvement in a participant friendly manner, using simple sentences, picture exchange mechanisms and illustrations to convey the information. For the participants that had difficulties in reading or had visual impairments, parents/carers or staff were asked to read the information leaflet to the participants. However, individualising information in this way proved to be costly, time consuming and challenging. Overcoming barriers, financial implications and time constrictions offer further explanations as to why disabled children and young people are often excluded from research, for it seems that those whose voices are more conventional and easier to gather are more readily accepted, included and, as a result are privileged.

Despite parent/carers consenting to their child's participation in research, gaining the children's consent from the outset is of vital importance, for as Taylor (1998) suggests, this takes seriously the need for upholding their rights and including them in decision-making processes. However, having researched with adults with learning disabilities, Simons et al. (1989) warn that disabled people have a tendency towards acquiescence because so much of their life is controlled by others. The same consideration can, however, be applied to many institutional contexts. We argue that different contexts produce specific responses and influence voices in particular ways. There is the potential for less adult-controlled social settings such as a playground to provide different responses to a particular issue than a highly authoritarian setting such as school classroom (for example, Punch 2002; Westcott and Littleton 2005). However, we are also aware of the power that children can exercise within adult-controlled spaces in ways that may not often be recognised or that are given credit for, such as the use of silence, as discussed in Chapter 2. Critical exploration of both physical and virtual space allows for a greater understanding of the power relations that flow within the various institutions of childhood both in general and research encounters and relationships.

Indeed, while Allison questioned whether those who were helped to complete the consent form did actually fully make the decision to participate independently, she also found that self-advocacy was problematic with non-verbal children who gave her informed consent independently, for it is often the case that children with little or no speech were taught to respond to promptings rather than initiate communication themselves. The following extract of a research conversation with a teaching assistant offers an enlightening perspective:

Matthew is very good at initiating conversations, but he doesn't do it very often. I think a lot of students are so used to having a passive role in life. Life just happens to them and they sit and it passes them by. They lose the habit of initiating things. Matthew can do it very well if he chooses to, and he chooses to quite often, but not as often as we would like

This reminds us that there is also a vital distinction between prompted and spontaneous communication whereby prompted communication allows participant's to respond to agendas and concerns of others, whereas spontaneous communication allows free expression which stems from the things that the children themselves feel are most important. Indeed, Potter and Whittaker (2001) found that prompt-based approaches encouraged passive responses from actors rather than active responses from agents who express their own needs and exert control over their environments as self-determined individuals. In order to address the ebb and flow of the participants understanding within Allison's study, their continuing consent was sought throughout the fieldwork in consideration for the sensitive recognition of the issues of power, voice and representation. This, she believed, resulted in the maintenance of respectful research relationships based on informed consent.

While issues of prompting and passivity are particularly explicit in Allison's research, they are however, pivotal ethical considerations in all research with children. This is because children cannot and should not be abstracted from the social context within which they are embedded with all the associated disciplinary regimes, power relations, opportunities and constraints that come with it. With this in mind, we argue that hearing the 'pure' voice of the child is an inherently problematic and flawed ideal.

### Critical reflexivity and children in research

While upholding rights of participation and pondering on how best to include children in research, Spyrou (2011) suggests that critical, reflexive researchers should reflect on the processes which influence children's positionality. He stresses that when we include children in research, we must not only be mindful of issues of representation, but also of the power imbalances that shape their voices and the contexts which inform them. As suggested previously, when we include their voices, we should also move beyond claims of authenticity by exploring the messy, multi-layered complexities that make up their voices. Indeed, Allison found that in order to include disabled children with little or no speech in her research she needed to deconstruct the popular notion of voice and pay particular attention to the ambiguity of it. The young participants adopted a vast range of communication methods, not necessarily associated with the common notion of 'voice'. For example, information leaflets and consent forms most commonly include a statement that outlines participant's right to withdraw from the research at any time. However, Allison was mindful that some participants may have forgotten this or they might not have fully understood it. In addition, while some of the participants were able to communicate their desire to withdraw, others did not have the vocabulary to enable them to do so. Therefore, she found that by considering voice as social and co-constructed instead of straightforward or linear. Allison looked for 'clues' as to how the participants were feeling and judge if the questions, observations or her very presence became intrusive. When trying to capture one young person's story, an incident occurred whereby pupils started filing past the classroom, distracting the participant. The sound of a distant bell indicated that it was break time. The participant indicated that he wished to terminate the interview:

Justin: 'Off' [pre-programmed response]
Allison: 'Off? You want me to turn this off?' [pointing to the tape recorder]
Justin: 'Yes' [and nods]
Allison: 'Ok' [I switch the machine off]

Pause

Justin: 'Bag' [pre-programmed response]
Allison: 'You want me to put it in my bag?'
Justin: 'Yes. Thank you' [pre-programmed response]
Allison: 'No worries' [I put the recorder back into the bag]
Justin: 'Classroom' [pre-programmed response]
Allison: 'You want to go back to your classroom?'
Justin: 'Yes' [pre-programmed response; and nodded]
Allison: 'Ok, give me a mo...' [I put my notepad and pen into my bag]...'Thank you for taking part in the interview, Justin.' [after confirming that he wanted me to, I took him back to the classroom]

Later and before the interview was transcribed, Allison reflected on the ambiguity of the situation. Did the participant want to withdraw completely from the research, withdraw momentarily or withdraw his consent to use the material? After much deliberation, she approached the young participant and asked him if he wanted to withdraw from the study. He was clearly amused. Their ensuing conversations revealed that being interviewed during break time was much less important to him than joining his friends for their usual game of wheelchair football! He confirmed that he had not intended to withdraw; he just wanted to 'go out to play'. On reflection, Allison realised that while the new orthodoxy of children's participation advocates providing opportunities for children and young people to be included, to express their views and explore the options open to them. Such perspectives are however, merely the beginning of hearing the voices of children and as discussed momentarily in Chapter 4, notions of child-centred research remain under-interrogated. While we do advocate the importance of listening, research encounters are rarely this simple. Voices are shaped not only by our views as researchers (for example, to listen carefully to the views of children) but crucially by the social context, the positioning of the individuals involved in the encounters and the fluidity of power relations that produce such conversations and as a consequence co-construct such knowledge.

## Conclusion

If we are truly interested in childhoods and wish to gain meaningful insights into children's lives in an ethical way, we should position ourselves as adults who wish to seek the knowledge of children, who want to learn what children know and show them that we genuinely want to learn from them (Mayall 2000b). However, upholding the participatory rights of disabled children and young people and including them in research is a tricky business. It calls for a unique and carefully considered approach for we believe that children's voices are multi-layered and it takes time to collect and understand them. Rushing in and out of children's worlds to quickly collect data and then shape it to fit and illustrate researchers own agendas simply won't do.

While we acknowledge that the discussions in this chapter draw heavily on research with disabled children and young people, we argue that the key issues raised are also of particular relevance to those wishing to give serious and critical ethical consideration to children's rights to participate. Undoubtedly, while the notion of universal rights offers a possible basis for cohesion in the face of fragmentation and diversity, in reality the plausibility of child agents actively engaging with them is minimal given their literal and metaphoric lack of voice. Indeed, as Morris argues, research with disabled children should place considerable significance on the study of the social arrangements surrounding rights, the way in which they 'function in relation to social structures and institutions, the way in which rights are accrued in particular areas by particular social groups and the contexts in which they are implemented and given meaning' (2006:243). In addition, real consequences for individuals require further consideration of rights issues in terms of how they are embedded within a society and its institutions (Stones 2005). Therefore, it is concluded that the principles and practices of rights in situ relate directly to opportunities made available to give individuals a voice and include them in research.

# 4
# The Illusion of Autonomy: From Agency to Interdependency

## Introduction

This chapter explores the influence on research that the contemporary emphasis on children's agency and autonomy has had and evaluates the usefulness of such terms in research-based contexts. We begin by outlining how agency and autonomy have become part of the social construction of childhood. We then consider the development of participant-led approaches to research with children, before evaluating the attribution of agency and autonomy to children, characteristics traditionally assumed to be the properties of adulthood (Lee 1999:458) yet currently promoted and pursued extensively in research with children. In this chapter, we question the appropriateness of the emphasis on these concepts and ask if alternative values might be more appropriate to reflect the roles of children in research as negotiated, relational and interdependent. If, as Parry (1991:180) contends, 'it is not possible to abstract from ourselves all our natural and social bonds, allegiances and commitments and still understand ourselves' then are concepts such as autonomy and agency require an independent selfhood relevant in research endeavours which seek to understand more about the social worlds of children? We identify and discuss ways in which children negotiate power relations within these social contexts which rely less on the skills of autonomy and more on establishing and negotiating social relations.

This chapter uses data examples to illustrate children as being socially embedded. We argue that greater recognition of interdependency in research relationships would enable a shift in ethical approaches from the current emphasis on agency of the individual to a focus on research relationships, emphasising nurturance and an ethic of care. These conversations begin with an outline of how agency and autonomy came to be so integral to contemporary childhood.

## Constructing the child as being in social research

The sociology of childhood initially emerged to challenge assumed notions of passivity and objectification of children. The social construction of childhood was premised on dependence and vulnerability, and the prevailing emphasis was on a 'becoming' child yet to acquire the skills associated with adulthood. In contrast, the sociology of childhood emphasised the agentic and 'being' child, and these ideas transformed how childhood could be perceived and how children might be regarded (James and James 2004; James et al. 1998; Jenks 1996; Qvortrup et al. 1994). The concept of the being child challenged notions of passivity and recognised instead the agency in children rather than the necessity of maturation for agentic development to occur.

The impact of this paradigm shift should not be underestimated, and in the field of social research into childhood it would be hard to overstate. However, more broadly, the emphasis on the 'being' child to the exclusion of other states has now been questioned. Gallacher and Gallagher (2008:510) argue that the notion of the child as 'becoming' has fallen prey to currently dominant ideas about the child as 'being' as a more appropriate discourse through which to reveal the realities of children's lives. As they put it, the idea of the child as 'becoming' has 'almost been vilified' (Gallacher and Gallagher 2008:510). Uprichard (2010) contends that the current emphasis on the child constructed as 'being', neglects a reality of the child as 'becoming', when children themselves frequently demonstrate knowledge and awareness of this state. Ignoring this aspect of childhood experience, she argues, places generated knowledge on a par with that created through the previously dominant construction of the child as 'becoming'. It offers a partial rather than complete picture, and Uprichard (2010) contends that both concepts are necessary to reveal childhood as lived by children. Gallacher and Gallagher

(2008:510) posit that the term 'becoming' itself needs to be redefined. They claim that the term need not be inextricably linked to predetermined developmental stages of childhood. But rather, that it is preferable to see childhood and adulthood in a 'present and continuous tense', where both adult and child are always emerging, unfinished and therefore becoming subjects. It is as part of this emerging critical evaluation of the perspectives held within the sociology of childhood that we situate this chapter where we use examples of our research experiences to review the dependence/independence dichotomy with particular reference to the concept of autonomy, its acquisition and its role in the research process. Here, we argue that the self of child and adult emerges through social relations in social contexts including our research endeavours.

Scientific and political interests in childhood and children have been evident for some considerable time, linked to modernisation of the nation state through industrialisation and the changing social and political need (Parton 2006; Prout 2005). Punch (2002) argues that perceptions about childhood and the status of children influence the ways in which research occurs. The contingent normative ideas of the time saw increasing perception of childhoods and their differentiation from adulthood (Qvortrup 1994). The social and political interest in this 'othered' state is inextricably linked to the methodological approach and research themes pursued. Educational and developmental exploration from medical and psychological disciplines has historically dominated research on children and into childhood. Such perspectives were aimed at gaining knowledge about the 'normal' developing child. Though mostly positivistic in approach, in aspiring to objectivity and neutrality, values and assumptions about childhood are nevertheless evident. Childhood as natural and becoming, following gender-specific roles and behavioural characteristics have been dominant features of research. Until recently, these assumptions have tended to be overlooked in academic literature (James and James 2004). Research, at times intrusive and alienating, focused mainly on the progression of the child towards rationality and physical and cognitive maturation (Elbers 2004), the developmental path towards the autonomous individual. Knowledge in how to assist this progression coupled with enquiry about the factors that might inhibit developmental progress has represented the majority of disciplines surrounding childhood. These interests are related to, and driven by, the social and political need to control and construct childhoods to produce an effective adult citizenry sufficient to the changing needs of the state (Cockburn 1998; Garrett 2009; Lange and Mierendorff 2009).

The objectification and homogenisation of childhood in these traditional stances, arguably neglected to acknowledge the child as a social actor with expertise in their social and cultural worlds, preferring instead the social construction of passive, dependent and vulnerable children, frequently categorised children as objects of concern or threat (Hendrick 2005). Also neglected were the social and cultural worlds of children (Christensen and Prout 2002). Recent emphasis on the rights of children, informed by the UNCRC legislation and academic discussions surrounding what is termed 'new sociology of childhood' (James and James 2004; Prout 2005), has played a significant role in ensuring children's individual subjectivity be recognised. Rights legislation has required that children's voices be heard in decisions made about their lives. Such changing ideas about children have caused a significant shift in how children and their childhoods are researched and have produced a diverse and changing methodological landscape. It has also shifted the role of individual children within research (Kellett et al. 2004). Complex and diverse social realities of children have emerged through alternative research methods. This methodological approach has matured and is now firmly established as an ethical way to conduct social research with children. The time for critically evaluative debate which moves the methodology forward has clearly arrived. Part of this emerging debate involves a greater interrogation of concepts embedded in this methodology such as agency and autonomy. Emirbayer and Mische (1998:962) have previously identified that not only the concept of agency is increasingly 'contradictory' and 'strained', but the term itself remains 'elusive and vague'. Yet agency, its pursuit and practice in childhood remains canonical with, as yet, little attempt to interrogate its meaning or appropriateness in children's lives, or indeed our research activities with them.

## Autonomy and its place in ethics

Autonomy in adulthood can be defined as being an individual who is 'self-sufficient, self-reliant and self-realizing', motivated by personal gain whose independence is threatened by other self-serving individuals (Walter and Ross 2014:16). This notion of autonomy is termed as the 'in-control model' (Walter and Ross 2014). Agency is intricately linked with the capacity to be autonomous and is associated with 'selfhood, motivation, will, purposivenss, intentionality, choice, initiative, freedom and creativity' (Emirbayer and Mische 1998:962). The 'in-control' model assumes and values rationality, sensible decision making and self-reliance, rather than a susceptibility towards the influence of others, referred to by Emirbayer and Mische (1998:965) as being 'freedom and rational self-interest'. There is an explicit emphasis in autonomy and agency on individual rights and self-protection (Greenfield 1994). Rose (1999:91) argues that this 'self' is 'an object of knowledge and autonomy' developed through a continuous process of self-improvement achieved by applying and privileging 'rational knowledge', the emerging autonomous self. This process enables individuals to constitute themselves as the 'self' required by contemporary society and government. Autonomy is dominant in a hierarchy of characteristics evident within an adult rights holder in advanced liberal societies and is regarded as a necessary component of economic citizenry (Tronto 2009:164). Unsurprising then that it is a characteristic that we expect children to acquire.

Autonomy has also been a dominant principle of ethics through the promotion of rights, protection of the individual and their capacity to make decisions and to engage in activities that individual actors find meaningful (Mullin 2014; see also Dworkin 1988). Its relationship with individualism is explicit. Code (1991) argues that this definition of autonomy has become closely aligned with a neo-liberal model of individualism where its virtues are privileged (Walter and Ross 2014) and inform ethical processes surrounding research. However, this independent individual is not a universal truth but is, as Greenfield (1994) reminds us, a particular cultural script for the development of the ideal person. There has been, according to Emirbayer and Mische (1998:963), a 'consistent failure' to recognise agency as temporally situated and emerging in social relations through social interaction. We argue that this failure to account for social interaction has had specific impact on ethical discourses concerning research with children, where the privileging of individual rights and selfhood remain pivotal in methods which promote participatory methodologies. The embedded contradiction here ensures that the ways in which children exert agency in research contexts is over-looked, even discounted as it risks undermining certain 'cherished conceits' (Segal 1999) in research such as objectivity and neutrality and the importance of a distanced researcher.

Significant contemporary focus is placed upon the rights of children. To be heard, to participate and to exert agency are all part of the discourse of contemporary childhood. The agency being fostered within the social institutions which surround children reflect ethical principles found in human rights legislation and are emphasised in ethical frameworks through which social research with children is conducted. These codes of behaviour are based upon the Cartesian subject where the rights of selfhood and individualism are integral. Children are assumed to have not yet developed characteristics associated with the 'in control model' but are encouraged to acquire these skills as they mature. This goal of future autonomy (Feinberg 1980) influences the expectation that children will now participate in meaningful decision making in their own lives and the lives of their communities. Indeed, agency – as being the ability to act independently – is a concept which has become a canonical narrative, a 'cherished conceit' (Segal 1999) if you will, in the social construction of childhood. Reflecting the need to acquire the skills associated with autonomy, Greenfield (1994) has argued that schools in neo-liberal and individualistic societies are structured around competitive models where individualism is valued and fostered. Within institutions such as the school and the family, an assumption of the dependent child being encouraged to move towards independent adulthood predominates. The role of parents to recognise the need for this developmental process (Killen and Wainryb 2000) and facilitate the acquisition of autonomy for their children is part of the cultural script. Individualism, agency and autonomy are required in contemporary adult citizenship; children are therefore expected to acquire the skills ready for adulthood. Research participation is just one arena for those skills to be practised. Yet participation constructed as a right of children can perhaps too easily become a responsibility. Within research with children terms such as autonomy and agency are used interchangeably and are taken to be a reflection of the more insightful and ethical approach to the social positioning of children in contemporary research. Such terms populate research texts generally but are rarely interrogated to determine their appropriateness. Yet, despite this emphasis on agency, children remain commonly consigned to the margins of ethical debates. Children's assumed incapacity to demonstrate autonomy is used as justification for this marginalisation (Richards 2012a). Indeed, many argue that child-centred research continues to be premised on long-standing assumptions of dependence and vulnerability (see, for example, discussions of assent versus informed consent in Chapter 2 of this volume).

Societies that value independence in adulthood assume the developmental journey to it begins with dependence in childhood. Self-protection as part of how independence and autonomy are perceived (Greenfield 1994) ensures that protecting not yet independent or autonomous children is an imperative aspect of the cultural script and consequently explicit in ethical processes. This presence of both protection and autonomy in ethical procedures creates another contradictory tension where child-centred methodologies call for an independent and agentic child to be at the forefront, while an autonomous rights discourse emphasises the need to protect those who lack the skills needed to protect themselves. In consequence, both characteristics are required and somewhat clumsily attributed to children by adults at various points throughout the research process. Sarah's ethics application is a case in point.

Methodologically, Sarah's research was premised on elevating the voices of young transracial intercountry adoptees, frequently excluded from debates about their adopted status (Richards 2013). Her first hurdle was getting ethical approval from the university to conduct the research. This took six months and a number of amendments to the proposal before eventually gaining approval from the faculty ethics committee. Sarah was requested to articulate her ability to manage researching a sensitive topic, and care for the vulnerable children involved. In the end, the research proposal emphasised children's agency and participation and their capacity to speak about life experiences while her ethical section and university application form spoke of the care of vulnerable children involved in a sensitive topic. This experience demonstrates that despite the impact that child-centred approaches to research are said to have had the combination of the need to both protect children and ensure their participation can still generate anxiety and inevitably produce contradictory constructions of childhood in locations where we generate knowledge.

In addition to producing contradictory expectations, the autonomy embedded within our dominant cultural script and ascribed to children through individual rights discourses, impedes recognition of relational or social agency achieved within the interdependency and inter-subjectivity of children's lives. Despite the plethora of discussions of child-centred research (Alderson 1995; Alderson and Goodey 1996), and newly emerging critical consideration of such methods, we argue that for the most part these approaches fall short because they too frequently seek agency and the voices of children in the 'wrong space' (Cockburn 2005). Child-centred methodologies can often focus on a decontextualised child within an autonomous and individualised space: the autonomy of selfhood (Walkerdine 1999). Greenfield (1994) argues that the individualism fostered in this cultural script is to the detriment of cooperation and community. We argue that it is also an inappropriate perspective to view the agency in children's social lives. MacIntyre (1981 in Parry 1991:182) contends that

> an essential element in the story of one's life is the community into which one is born, or is brought up ... these give a person's life its own moral particularity ... the story of my life is always embedded in the story of those communities from which I derive my identity.

As social individuals we require a society which allows us opportunities to cultivate our social competencies (Twine 1994). Competencies such as agency, autonomy, and morality, should therefore be seen as an expression of the social (Frankel 2012) rather than the individualised self. The autonomous self depicted by Rose (1999:91) as emerging through a continuous process of self-improvement is, we argue as Twine (1994) does, achieved through knowledge acquired in social relations. A dynamic self who constantly re-shapes and repositions their 'self' depending on the social context they are in and the power they can exert in it (Frankel 2012). A social self, emerging from our social relationships through a dynamic of 'choice and constraint' and thus never fully autonomous nor fully determined (Twine 1994:11), the being and becoming self. It is this social and relational agency in children's research experiences that we explore next.

## Children's relational agency

Just as independence or individualism is part of an idealised cultural script, so too is interdependence, also referred to as 'collectivism' (Greenfield 1994:7). Each script stems from alternative 'philosophies of life' (ibid.), where Western cultures have commonly privileged individualism, many Asian cultures value interdependence. In contrast to a Western script an idealised Asian cultural script presumes that children begin developmentally as independent individuals and must be taught and allowed to develop the skills of interdependence (Greenfield 1994). Here selfhood is achieved not through autonomy or individualism but through relational subjectivity with family and community. Montgomery's (2007) research with child prostitutes in Thailand successfully articulates the expectation and responsibility of children to foster interdependent relationships with family and community. Of course each us are both individuals and members of social groups and so both are inextricably linked in the ways that we live our lives. The point is that the particular script which is culturally emphasised and idealised influences how the development of children is organised and determines what is appropriate in their lives and what is not. The balance between independence and interdependence is determined by whichever concept is most highly valued. The ideal adult citizen is then constructed as holding this characteristic. Both concepts have strengths and limitations. Simplistically one places the social above the individual and the other values the individual above the collective. However, by placing such value on independence, individualism and autonomy we risk overlooking children's capacity for relational agency. This oversight ensures that the ways in which children exert themselves and achieve their goals through and within the social context is often neglected.

A relational concept of autonomy is not overlooked entirely however. In contrast to previous clarifications of agency and autonomy which idealise an independent selfhood, Emirbayer and Mische (1998:970) define human agency as being, 'the temporally constructed engagement by actors of different structural environments – the temporal – relational contexts of action'. Such a perspective is premised upon people being 'socially embedded' where our personalities and identities emerge within social relationships in our social contexts (Mackenzie and Stoljar 2000). This 'intrinsically social and relational' agency is achieved through the 'engagement and disengagement' of actors in their contextual environments, which Emirbayer and Mische (1998:973) refer to as 'structured yet flexible social universes'. This relational model of autonomy refutes the existence of the 'in control' model individual, as discussed earlier. We place this relational agency, this interdependency, at the forefront of the following empirical accounts.

Using a perspective of interdependency between participant and researcher we potentially enhance the visibility of children as socially connected with moral agency and power (Malaguzzi 1993). This representation of childhood produces children as active in reciprocal relationships rather than the abstract individual commonly found in the language of autonomy, rights and ethics. Seeing these children allows us to move beyond research where a dominant theme is that of the right to protection, too often premised on the weak and vulnerable child, whose right to self-protection as an autonomous self is not yet fully developed, and instead, listen to socially situated and connected children (Richards 2013). Recognising the relational connections between individuals in the research process can be challenging. Detachment and neutrality may be the traditional language of positivistic experimental methods (Smith 2005), but it is not necessarily the language of children's or indeed adult's worlds (Richards 2013).

As we discuss in Chapter 2, research with children now commonly takes place in environments familiar to the children: nursery, home, school being typical examples (Harden et al. 2000; Lewis et al. 2004). These places are assumed to be locations where children feel safe and are more likely to contribute effectively (Harden et al. 2000). Nevertheless, research with children in these social settings holds particular dilemmas, both social and ethical. What it can reveal however, are the ways in which children negotiate relations and exert relational agency. In Sarah's research, the young participants frequently placed Sarah in different roles during the data collection activities. For example, casting Sarah in a teacher role was quite common. She found herself variously having to spell words, comment on neatness of writing, and to determine or confirm whether an answer was a correct one. Despite being uncomfortable in this role and its contrast with her methodological values, Sarah complied in the interests of maintaining good relations and collecting data. Waller and Bitou (2011) claim that current methods often used in participatory research with children induce such pedagogical relations. A young participant called Wim (aged eight years) confirmed her perception of the similarity between Sarah and a teacher throughout the interview by her continued compliance and deferral to her in decision making, and also through requests for guidance in spelling and for what she should write in order to address correctly the pages in the activity book she was given. The following questions are typical of ones that she asked having verbally told a story and needing confirmation that it would be appropriate to a specific page that had instigated the telling of the story:

'Can I put what I used to call my mummy here?'

...

'Shall I put that here?'

Throughout the interview Wim sought approval for each contribution made and exerted her social agency by ensuring that Sarah fulfil this role. Little wonder perhaps that when at the outset of the activity with Wim, Sarah suggested, 'you are in charge', Wim simply laughed. This interaction demonstrates that Wim's understanding of the power relations contrasted with Sarah's, and her laughter related more to her perception of Sarah's foolishness in suggesting that it was anything other than the usual adult/child power relation, rather than evidence of a growing rapport that she took it to be at the time. In this instance, Wim grasped the reality of the situational dynamics and Sarah, as the researcher was innocent in relation to them. The dialogue demonstrates the tension between how researchers may assume and wish agency to be and how it actually emerges in social contexts. The implicit resistance on the part of Wim to assume the powerful role, but still to remain on good terms with Sarah as the adult and yet comply with other aspects of this interaction, demonstrates complex, agentic and successful negotiation of the adult spaces in which she was placed and challenges simplistic notions of agency and selfhood.

Walkerdine (1989:270) argues that the teacher (like the mother) becomes the facilitator in the learning environment, not there to instruct but to observe in a more passive role in contrast to the active roles that are performed by the child. Adults here, like the adults in child-centred research, take a 'nurturant, facilitating, sensitive and supportive role' where intervention but not interference is required. Walkerdine argues that these approaches are founded on an 'illusion of autonomy and control' (ibid). However, we claim that the relationship with participants in this facilitative and nurturing role does not negate children's autonomy but demonstrates an alternative social understanding of the concept and therefore challenges contemporary ideas of pursuing the traditional model of autonomy in research into childhood.

The capacity to be agentic develops within dynamic, situated contexts and is always in a state of re-evaluation and reconstruction on the part of the actors involved (Schutz 1962). Sarah variously demonstrated throughout the fieldwork, ascribed characteristics of 'mother', 'teacher' and 'researcher'. At times she performed the role of teacher because her participants cast her as such as they negotiated their way through the activity. At other times, she performed 'the good researcher with children' through aspirations of empowerment, capturing the voices of young participants, and on occasion, ensuring that their right to withdraw, remain silent, or leave stories untold, was protected in the face of frustration from their parents. These roles were not selected at random but came about as part of ongoing interaction with participants. The girls cast these roles which Sarah duly performed, in part to connect with them but also to illicit and encourage their participation in the research. A simplistic focus on 'selfhood' in research with children misses the significance of the network of relations, peer, family and wider social networks that situate and inform children's lives and research relations.

Despite Sarah's desire to ensure the voices of the young participants were at the forefront of the discussions on their intercountry adoptions, the voices of others within the family also shaped the data collected. While this complicated the ownership of the stories, it also revealed the social position of children within the home and provided insight into research conducted in the home (see Chapter 2). The following account taken from Sarah's research

(Richards 2013) demonstrates the 'messiness' of these research relationships.

> One family made the dining room and table available to me to run the activity with the two daughters taking part. There were two doors to the room, one led to the kitchen and one to the living room. The room was therefore used like a connecting corridor from kitchen to living room. The doors were pulled closed by the mother as I began to talk to the two girls. As lunch time drew close however, (and I had already been invited to join them and as a guest felt obliged to say 'yes'), both parents began to walk through the room and then the mother (in particular) stopped to glance at the books that the girls were making as part of the data collection, and make the occasional suggestion about content. At the end of the interview she came in to say that lunch was ready. As I cleared away the pens and glue, Janet (mother) asked to read the journals which were still on the table. This request was difficult to respond to, the journals belonged to the girls, and this had been made clear to them at the outset. To acquiesce would contradict their ownership, and to refuse would be rude in their home, prior to sitting down and eating lunch and before interviewing the parents, already identified as potentially problematic in the establishment of rapport and guest relations. I suggested that if the girls agreed to show their journals then I was happy for them to do so. The girls, perhaps unsurprisingly, agreed and their mother sat down at the dining table and read through each page. She commented on handwriting, spelling, and the content of some stories and the absence of others which she felt that the girls could have or should have included. On occasion she added written comments onto the pages, which she felt were relevant or where her daughter(s) had not written anything on. The Figures 4.1 & 4.2 illustrate this.

Whatever our individual expectations or aspirations of what participatory research with children might be, we cannot remove children from the social context that they occupy or separate their voices from the intergenerational power relationships: the 'constraints and choices' (Twine 1994:11) through which they live their lives. Nor should we attempt this if we really wish to capture their life experiences.

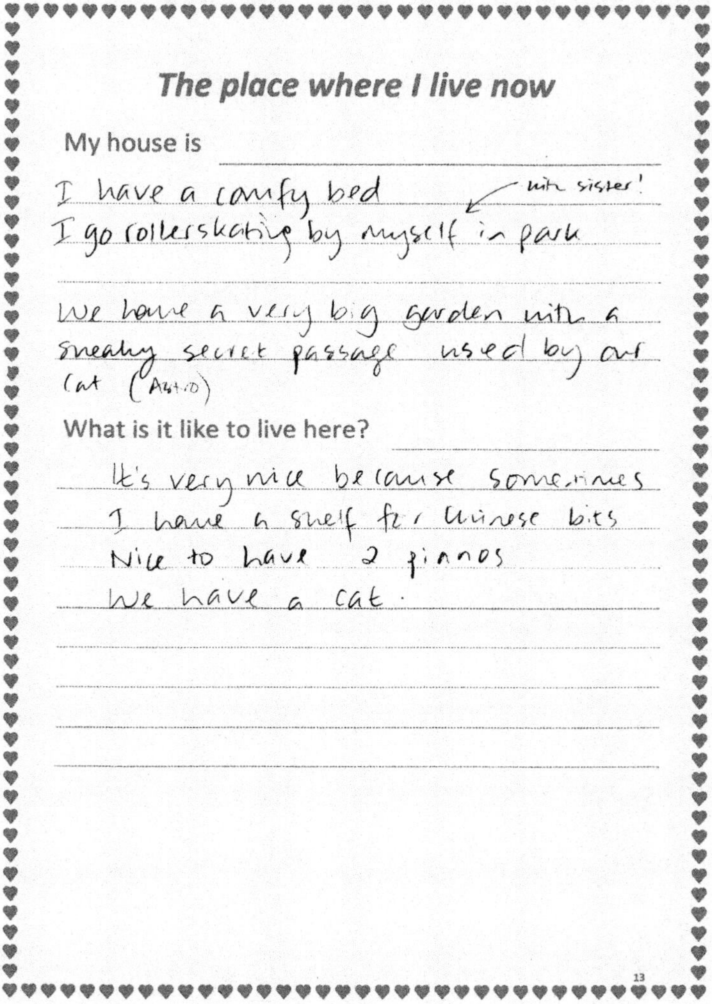

> ### The place where I live now
>
> My house is _____
>
> I have a comfy bed ————— with sister!
> I go rollerskating by myself in park
>
> We have a very big garden with a
> sneaky secret passage used by our
> cat (Austin)
>
> **What is it like to live here?**
>
> It's very nice because sometimes
> I have a shelf for Chinese bits
> Nice to have 2 pianos
> We have a cat.

*Figure 4.1*  The place where I live now

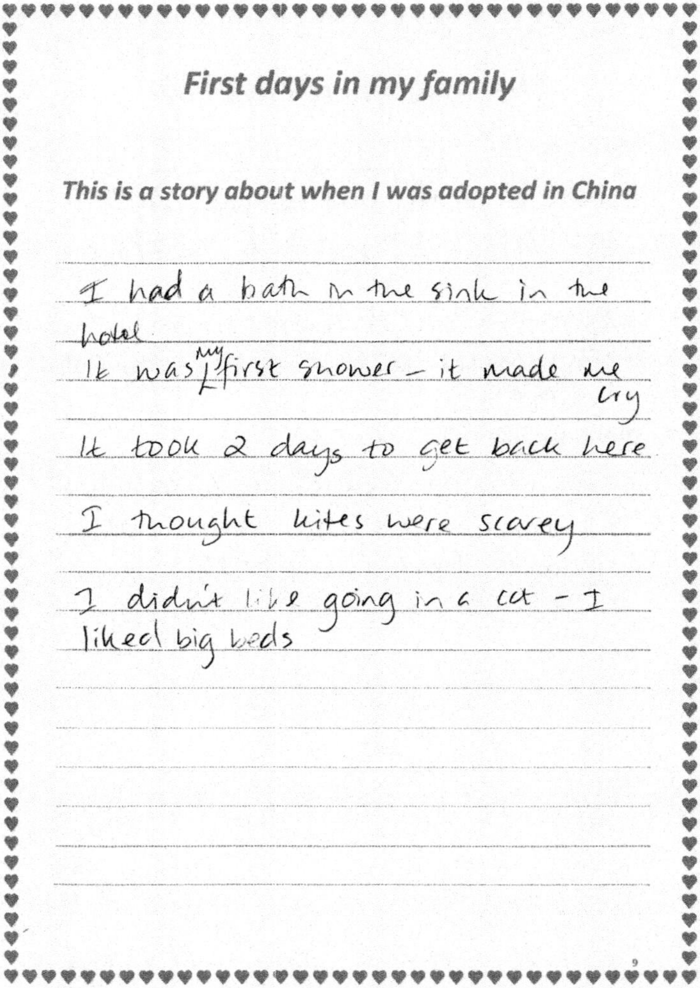

92

### First days in my family

**This is a story about when I was adopted in China**

I had a bath in the sink in the hotel

It was my first shower – it made me cry

It took 2 days to get back here

I thought kites were scarey

I didn't like going in a cot – I liked big beds

*Figure 4.2* First days in my family

Consider the following examples from Sarah's research which illustrate the ways in which family members co-construct their own stories. Here are the experiences of a mother meeting her child for the first time:

> Sally: 'We arrived and were told we were going to meet her the following day and then there was a knock at the hotel door and the guide was there and he said, 'baby coming in half an hour', so it was a bit of a shock and we were jet lagged and hungry. And half an hour later she was at the door screaming. They handed her to me and she went very quiet and was looking around to see where the orphanage director and carer was but she was not crying. But after they had gone she just latched onto my husband and decided to only go to him. The rest of the week that we were in China she would not come to me.'

Ricoeur (1991) suggests that stories are performed for particular social contexts and are therefore different each time with multiple and changing key aspects as story lines. First meetings are the important initial stories of belonging told by adopters. They are told to the girls to help them begin to comprehend where and to whom they belong as a result of adoption. The girls speak of the same events and similar key figures, but with alternative explanations. In the account below, Sally relies on a specific narrative within this adoption group about subordinate approaches to care within the orphanages. She implies that this care varies from what she and her husband begin to provide, and suggests that this is why their daughter initially rejects her. She gave this response after she had disclosed that her daughter had refused to let her hold her until they had returned to the UK and Sarah asked her how she felt about it.

> Sally: 'Um, it was okay, it must have all been really so strange and I did wonder at the time whether it was because I had blue eyes and must look very different. And we knew someone going out at a similar time said that she felt the children were only picked up by the orphanage director who was a man and that maybe the women did not have enough time to pick the girls up and cuddle them, so we considered that this was a possibility as well. I was told that there were ten babies to a room with one carer so it

must have been quite busy. Whether it was that kind of thing or whether my difference in colouring or both, I'm not sure. But obviously we knew it was going to be really, really strange. She eventually let me give her a chocolate biscuit and that was fine.'

While mothers speak of strangeness, and rationalise rejection, the girls construct similar but differing stories, positioning themselves as babies to explain their rejection of their adoptive parents. Wim (Sally's daughter) tells her version of the same story:

> Wim: 'When I was in China, I was a baby so I don't really know what happened. I didn't like Mummy so Daddy had to carry me when we were in China. But when we got back home, Mummy gave me a chocolate biscuit and I liked her then [she laughs] Mummy thinks it was because Daddy had darker eyes and Mummy has light blue eyes and I might have been used to Daddy's colour eyes.'

In this different example, highlighted below we can also see how such important stories are co-constructed. Here, Lisa also recounts a story of initial rejection by her towards her parents. Lisa's younger sister Jane interjects to explain her elder sister's behaviour:

> Lisa: 'I cried. I remember when I kept stealing the biscuits. Well Mummy and Daddy gave me a biscuit and I ate it and then they gave [orphanage director] a biscuit and I took it because she was right next to me. They were pink ones.'
>
> Jane: 'You didn't understand. You were just a baby.'
>
> Lisa: 'My Mummy calls me Peaches because when she got me I had a hole in my bottom [split in trousers traditionally used in China] and when she held me for the first time she said it was as smooth as a peach.'

Being 'a baby' explains the inexplicable, the rejection of the parents they both now love and trust. Both girls laugh about this response to their parents and use humour in telling how the eldest also got her family nickname. Lisa claims these accounts as her memories. This perhaps is not surprising as she has been told these stories over the six years since her adoption, and has seen the video of it taking place frequently. She has participated in the telling of the story with her family members (as does her younger sibling despite being absent, and not even born when the event took place) and thus here we see how such family stories are woven together into narratives of belonging (Richards 2013).

Acknowledgement that data is collected through these relationships causes us as researchers to confront epistemological issues in our research, to reflect on whose voices are being promoted and how we construct our analysis. The 'autonomous child' discourse so prevalent in participatory research allows for the decontextualised abstracted (Komulainen 2007) voices of children to be elevated at the expense of the socially embedded children. Consequently we lose their expertise in social contexts and their negotiation of social relations.

A further example in Sarah's research of the agency exerted through social interaction is provided by an account which again took place in the home where a mother stayed throughout the data collection with her two daughters. On occasion this mother prompted her daughters by reminding them that they had relevant information to complete the pages (and that she knew this because she had provided them with the stories). As discussed in detail in Chapter 2, in certain instances one of her daughters chose to remain silent. Her mother began to reprimand her daughter and made suggestions as to what could be put on the various blank pages. However, Jenny (aged 12) continued to refuse to complete certain pages, focusing instead on those in the book that could capture her contemporary friendships, travel aspirations, and, on occasion, challenge parental decisions about out of school activities, the lack of a family pet and holiday destinations.

Sarah grew concerned that Jenny may have been coerced into participating and so reiterated to both mother and daughter that leaving pages blank were perfectly acceptable as a response, and that stopping was also fine at any point. However, Jenny continued to complete other pages and talked at length with her sibling about what her sister was writing in her book. Interestingly, Jenny claimed authoritative knowledge of her younger sibling's unfolding adoption stories and corrected her on occasion in the interview, yet claimed to have no knowledge of her own. Sarah's concern about Jenny's informed consent was confirmed when in the subsequent interview with her mother, Linda revealed that her interest in participating had in part, been to try to find a way to get her daughter to talk about a subject that she was silent about within the family. At that point Sarah made the decision not to include Jenny's data. However, when she looked in detail at her book and listened to the recording of the data collection, it became apparent that Jenny had talked about things that she wanted to share and knew that her participation was on this basis. This left Sarah with a dilemma, to exclude the stories that Jenny had given on the basis that she was using the research to continue an ongoing challenge towards her mother was not a particularly ethical decision. Should Sarah exclude her voice? As a 12-year-old girl Jenny used this event to continue a family dynamic with her mother and had left pages blank clearly knowing that this was frustrating to her parent. Jenny's ability to both comply with her mother by taking part but continue to remain silent about a subject that her mother wished her to talk about demonstrates skills of autonomy within her social relations.

As a guest in this home, Sarah struggled to understand the unfolding social and political dynamics (Mayall 2000) and as a researcher she questioned and anguished over the ethical ramifications of what was taking place. Slote (2007) argues that parents, who allow for the individualities of children, demonstrate respect for their opinions and aspirations, ultimately, facilitate a nurturing environment for the acquisition of autonomous thinking. The home environment is clearly a location where children socially engage and practise autonomous thinking within social interactions. For researchers working in the homes of these children, autonomy and agency can become problematic to determine given the social situatedness of the children involved. The ethical implications for participatory research can present real dilemmas during data collection activities. The disconnect between the dominant definitions and applications of these terms and the ways that children practise them is not as yet well acknowledged. Greater recognition of the relationships and interdependencies of all those involved in the research process at the proposal and ethics application stage would better prepare researchers for the challenges that these can present in the field. The interdependencies of relationships, including that with the researcher, require an ethic of care (Cockburn 2005), an essential and as yet arguably neglected methodological aspect. A moral responsibility to care for the participants and the relationships forged and developed in the research is paramount rather than the adherence to a disconnected set of individualised rights and responsibilities. In this perspective, ethics are viewed as a principle of nurturance (Cockburn 2005), trust and negotiation (Richards 2012b, 2013).

## Conclusion

Within social interactions, the expected repertoire of adult/child relations allows the actors involved to predict behaviour associated with these particular identities (see also Chapter 5). This allows for consistent and coordinated social interaction. Yet improvisation on the part of the actors within these social contexts is constantly occurring (Tilly 1994). Children are aware of their expected roles, yet they demonstrate their capacity for evaluative judgement of their evolving social contexts and can be seen to be agentic in shaping these social situations to their advantage. Consider Wim's success in ensuring that Sarah played the role of teacher despite Sarah's wish that Wim make the decisions, or the expertise with which Jenny used silence as a strategy of resistance towards her mother.

Assuming a perspective of interdependence enables us to recognise the ways that children participate and the contribution they can make to social research. As we and others have previously argued, participation is not straightforward or progressive, and it cannot simply be elicited through application of a particular method alone (Waller and Bitou 2011), but it is always relational. Children are socially embedded, and terms such as 'autonomy' therefore ill-define their agency. An ethical stance which seeks to emphasise independent agency, inaccurately positions children and seeks to elevate their status inappropriately. An emphasis on interdependence in research would more effectively reflect the social positioning of children as social beings, not as autonomous agents, and provide a more effective way of promoting their participation ethics in research needs to focus more on the embedded nature of children's participation rather than the pursuit of agency or a rational autonomy.

The relationships that are frequently a focus of research are those within childhoods and amongst children, rather than the multiple, intergenerational relationships where children successfully collaborate with adults and which demonstrate the interdependencies of children and adults (Ennew 1994; Mayall 2000a).

The interdependency of adult and child, researcher and participant remain overlooked and yet key to understanding the context in which research with children is situated. Participant-led methodology should seek to undermine the binary logic between self and 'other' that plays such a key role in identity construction and the development of autonomy.

Being ethical in this perspective then is to achieve and sustain an awareness of the social context, the social agents, the power relationships and their influences on the research process. Working towards this requires both a personal reflexive approach towards subjective values and positioning as well as an epistemological one that explores the role of method in knowledge construction. Such reflexivity remains underexplored in much research (Madden 2010). Treading with care through these multiple relationships requires not only a reflexive approach but also an ethic of care.

We contend that to engage in research with children, we need to recognise more effectively the ways that children exert agency and negotiate power relations within their social contexts. Rather than autonomy of selfhood, children exhibit a relational social agency that has yet to be recognised in ethical frameworks. Such procedures continue to protect the vulnerable child while seeking to engage with an autonomous one. Such contradiction cannot be ethical nor reveal children's actual characteristics. As this chapter reveals, children exhibit agency in ways we may not expect or immediately recognise. But abstracting their voices from the social context and attributing autonomy denies the skilful ways that children manage relations as interdependent beings.

# 5
# Ramifications of Category Entitlement: In What Ways Does Who We Are Determine What Others Will Say?

## Introduction

The researcher-self as a significant presence in the field has become more prominent in research discussions but, though established, the issue remains contested in research debates. Our aim for this chapter is to acknowledge the presence of ourselves in our research and begin to explore the ways in which who we are shapes what we find and why we find it. We use a specific focus of category entitlement to explore the situated and connected category memberships of those involved in our own research with the express purpose of extending the debate beyond ideas that the researcher is influential, to explore how this influence is established and articulated.

Extensive literature is available which explores the role of the researcher in the field (see, for example, Wheatley 1994). Perhaps less is evident in how the researcher's subjectivity shapes the analysis of the data, with the possible exception of notable feminist arguments (Alvesson and Sköldberg 2009; Mauthner and Doucet 2003). In addition, limited literature is available which takes a reflexive perspective concerning the identity of the researcher and how their identity traits influence and shape the research process (Holstein and Gubrium 1995). Who takes part, what data they provide, how it is analysed and finally written up and presented is often overlooked. Debate around the extent to which the researcher shapes and influences the field (Coffey 1999), how they use subjective knowledge to illuminate the field in ways that objective observers cannot (Oakley 1981), or indeed whether they contaminate the field (Atkinson and Coffey 2003), are common but limited in their explorations.

To overemphasise our presence in research is a rather arrogant (Atkinson and Coffey 2003) and an essentialistic (Howarth 2002) position to assume. Yet to deny our position and its influence is illusionary (Mauthner and Doucet 2003; Sin 2005) and somewhat disingenuous. However, to actually recognise the extent of our influence in our own research is both challenging and time consuming and, if acknowledged, opens our research to scrutiny through diverse and contested values about validity and neutrality in the research process. Dunbar et al. (2002:131) challenge researchers not to treat interviewees as mere vessels from which stories can be abstracted and presented as objective facts devoid of the social and historical context in which they are told. They claim that this results in simplistic portrayals of complex social settings. We contend that the researcher producing this knowledge should not be abstracted from their social context either. Both interviewer and interviewee need to be acknowledged as situated participants, whose identities play a pivotal role in the research produced. Song and Parker (1995) claim that far more research is needed on how respondents and researchers establish identities in social research. What emerges if we study interviews through identity attributes are displays of cultural practices by its members (Silverman 1993:114) as they construct their identities.

It has been argued that identity and location cannot be erased in an attempt to 'clean up' data (Howarth 2002:29). Yet the expectation of objectivity is that such contaminants be removed or at the very least minimised. Holstein and Gubrium (1995:114) contend that active interviews should be built on the understanding that 'any attempt to strip interviews of their interactional ingredients will be futile'. Despite these and similar claims, published research frequently neglects to account for the attributes of those who collect data, where this is done and how. Differences, demographic and cultural between researchers and respondents are often ignored with the possible exception of some ethnographic studies (see, for example, Pole 2007) and yet these differences shape how accounts from respondents are understood and analysed (Poindexter 2003). We claim that similarities between respondents and researchers are equally neglected and yet play a significant role in the interview construction and subsequent analyses. This neglect not only reduces the epistemological richness of research based discussions but it also has ethical implications too. Fine (1994) argues that this separation of researcher and respondent contributes to the 'othering' of respondents and their experiences and produces narratives where researchers speak for others without acknowledging their own presence and investment in the final product (Poindexter 2003). This is perhaps particularly so in research which aims to elevate the voices of some groups such as children. We question the extent to which abstracted voices devoid of context successfully promote values of empowerment and participation espoused so frequently in participant led approaches with children.

This chapter explores the 'processes of production and interpretation' (Aull Davies 2008:110) of data by applying three connected topics that develop and use category entitlement to allow the influential identity traits of the researcher and respondent to be illustrated. Category membership, self-disclosure and insider status are all related to how individuals in social research establish relations and demonstrate their authority to speak on the issues researched. We detail the implicit and explicit connections established in the research context and consider the ways in which these connections build an entitlement on the part of the researcher to ask, understand and evaluate data as well as enable the respondent to establish a legitimacy to provide responses on a given topic. We also consider the ethical implications which become explicit when acknowledging the connections between researchers and researched. What we offer in this chapter is analysis of the relationships and identities which emerge and influence the research but which are frequently left out of published accounts. From this perspective all participants involved use personal histories, identities and subject positions (Phoenix 2008) at various stages of the research process to achieve diverse objectives and perform various roles. We focus on interviewer and interviewee identities and explore the influence of their category membership and entitlement on the data collection and analysis. Initially we clarify category membership and illustrate this outline with examples of transcripts from our own research.

## Category membership

Literature concerning the attribution of people to particular socially constructed categories is well established. Hacking (1986) for example, provides a comprehensive, philosophical discussion of the emergence of particular categories, and the 'making up' of people. He explores how categorisation 'affects our very idea of what it is to be an individual' (1986:161) and argues that the particular social and historical contexts in which categories such as 'pervert' or 'Parisian waiter', emerge, 'create new ways for people to be' (p.165). What individuals are able to be and do within these categories is inextricably linked to their description. Using Sartre's argument, Hacking compares these categories to imprisonment where our individual potential and possibilities are constrained by the category descriptions we are attributed to. Child, adult, researcher, adoptee, or disabled, for example, are categories of particular relevance in our discussion. Hacking contends that through the process of categorisation, experts or those with power, can create 'realities' or truths about groups of people but, that as individuals, we also have the capacity to resist such 'realities' (p.168). This perspective can easily be applied to social research where the researcher, often categorised as an expert, constructs realities about social groups and individuals through the research process.

It is argued that social categories are instrumental in much social research, often regarded as the 'principle building blocks' (Potter and Wetherell 1987:116). People are taken to be members of relatively enduring social categories. We each carry categorical labels, such as mother, father, teacher, adult, child, and are attributed characteristics accordingly. Potter and Wetherell (1987:137) argue that we each construct versions of the groups or collectivities to which we belong. These are then used to build and interpret our social worlds; however, these structures are neither solid nor static, but are shaped and adapted in each social interaction. Garfinkel (1967) and Sacks (1992) claim that there exists a range of culturally available knowledge, which we use to interpret and make sense of the actions of others and which inform our own actions and behaviour. This knowledge is embedded within social life, implicit and unnoticed but such

> categories are not nested in a clear-cut, natural way like Russian Dolls, for example, one inside another, but are grouped into collections by the use of potentially complex and contradictory sets of interpretative procedures
>
> (Potter and Wetherell 1987:128)

Sacks (1974) argues that people use knowledge of how categories are organised as a resource when making sense of discourse in the social world, which makes category membership an important research concept.

Individuals categorised as members of a particular group are associated with specific activities and attributes which enable them to make sense of their social environments. Category memberships enable each of us to make sense of the discourse and behaviour of others (Baker 2003; Sacks 1974; Silverman 1998). We use it to predict how people in that category will behave and what activities they will do. For example we can all predict some of the activities associated with a category of mother or child (Sacks 1974).

People specifically indicate their category memberships as part of their discourse and analysis of such conversational interaction is most highly developed in the field known as conversation analysis (CA). This approach originated in the work of Harvey Sacks, Emanuel Schegloff, and Gail Jefferson, is also closely related to ethnomethodology and accounts for how we make sense of each other and build knowledge through our category memberships. It is defined by Heritage (1984:4) as

the study of a particular subject matter: the body of common-sense knowledge and the range of procedures and considerations by means of which the ordinary members of society make sense of, find their way about in, and act on the circumstances in which they find themselves.

Baker (2003:395) contends that such analyses consider *how* participants make sense of each other, how knowledge is built, how identities are negotiated, and how participants 'characterize and connect the worlds they talk about'. Howarth (2002:23) argues that a 'theory that forges a link between what we say, who we are and where we are located, provides valuable inroads into epistemological debate'. Analysis of membership categorisation is described by Baker (2003:401) as being a 'powerful approach to uncovering the reflexive relation of speaker, audience, and topic in research interviews'. From this perspective interviews can be used to explore how participants claim membership and accomplish category entitlement to knowledge and experiences, and convey this through the interview process.

Yet examples of children using category membership in research is curiously absent.

Using categories in everyday discourse involves language, social expectations and attributes associated with membership of specific categories, which makes analyses of these membership categories highly relevant in research discussions. Category membership also provides the participants and researchers with authority to offer valid data collected in the interview process (Potter 1996). This is done by members claiming to hold 'expert knowledge or privileged experience' on research topics (Phoenix 2008:71).

Access to children can be challenging to achieve in a contemporary climate of concern about adults relations with children (for example, Monaghan et al. 2012). It is also one of the first ways that category membership can be explicit in the research process. To gain such access Sarah, in her research exploring intercountry adoption, used various category memberships. In the ethics application Sarah identified specific characteristics and qualifications each indicating specific knowledge and entitlements designed to enhance approval. Lecturer in childhood, qualified teacher, adoptive parent and bereavement counsellor were all specified, each category suggesting knowledge assumed to be pertinent to the topic and respondents and each making the ethics committee more comfortable for the research to proceed.

Having eventually gained ethical approval the process of recruitment began where category membership was also found to be influential. Despite a long-standing significance of values such as neutrality and objectivity (Poindexter 2003) in research discussions, participants are commonly selected on the basis of being members of a particular category and therefore holding specific and subjective knowledge relevant to the research topic (Howarth 2002). Baker (2003:401) argues that researchers recruit representative respondents using membership categories. Interviewees are then intended to sound like members of that category, speak from within that particular category and are accountable for speaking as competent members of that category. To encourage respondents to take part, researchers can also identify their membership to specific categories. For example in the information letter sent to parents, Sarah identified herself as a lecturer in Early Childhood Studies explicitly placing herself in a category where specific knowledge about children would be assumed. It also implied a position of trust to encourage parents to be more willing to agree to their child's participation. In the subsequent phone conversations Sarah identified herself as an intercountry adoptive mother where an element of trust might be implied through being an insider of this small and rather private group. Sarah also used her membership of this group to recruit participants at CACH (Children Adopted from China) events where only adoptive families were permitted to attend again explicitly situating herself as a member of the group that she wished to recruit from. While acknowledging the significance of objectivity in research debates Sarah, on reflection, purposefully and strategically used her membership categories to achieve specific outcomes in recruitment. We question the extent to which this is generally acknowledged in research and argue that there is a need for a greater reflection on how memberships can shape our recruitment strategies.

Notwithstanding the above arguments researchers also interpret interview data from within their roles (Rojiani 1994) and particular categories which makes these category memberships an important element of the research process. Poindexter (2003) argues that where we position ourselves determines our position on the topics we research. In accordance with this perspective we begin to explore more fully the role of self-disclosure where explicit examples of social actors establishing category membership are illustrated within the discourse. Challenges and opportunities which an insider status provides are then explored before evaluating the use of category membership in research relations upon which entitlement to contribute is established.

## Self-disclosure

The issue of self-disclosure is commonly absent in social research discussions and little attention has been paid to the interviewer's use of self-narratives of disclosure (Abell et al. 2006:223). Researchers can be concerned that to identify when and how they self-disclose in the field (if they have) may reduce the objectivity and impartiality of the data they collect and cast doubt on its validity. Such disclosure is often regarded as 'contamination' in conventional research (Dunbar et al. 2002:138). Holstein and Gubrium (1995:13) note that interviewers are generally expected to keep their 'selves' out of the interview process'. Consequently such accounts are cleansed from content where self-disclosure and connections between respondents and researchers have occurred leaving the complexity and ambiguity of these research relations underexplored.

To self-disclose is to offer a connection between the researcher and the researched, to invest in them as social beings (Dunbar et al. 2002). To actively self-disclose has been referred to as 'creative interviewing' where common but not necessarily comfortable ground can be established (ibid.). Abell et al. (2006:224) argue that interviewers activate category membership through self-disclosure in order to develop a rapport, or to identify a difference with respondents. Oakley (1981) argues that the researcher who is prepared to invest their personal identity in the relationship gains greater insight into the lives of those being researched in part because self-disclosure by the interviewer can also effectively facilitate further interview talk from the respondent (Abell et al. 2006). But to gather data as a result of such connection opens up complex epistemological debates.

Our data illustrates that children, like adults, are using categories to position themselves in the research context. Children can be seen to account for themselves as competent members of the social category assigned to them by the interviewer as well as claiming membership to categories that the interviewer has not assigned them. We consider examples where respondent's membership to specific categories is assumed by the interviewer (Phoenix 2008; Song and Parker 1995) but challenged by the interviewee:

Kate (nine years): 'Why do you want to talk to me just because I'm adopted?'

Sarah: 'I'd like to hear lots of your stories about friendships and about activities and school and I would also like to hear your adoption stories partly because we don't know much about these stories and partly because I have a daughter who was also adopted from China. She is still very little and I am interested in hearing what older girls think and feel about being adopted from China.'

Kate: 'What province is your daughter from?'

Sarah: [I name the province]

Kate: [with a look of surprise on her face] 'That's my province. I was born there too.'

Kate: [sits down on the floor next to her older sister, opens the activity journal and picks up a pen]
Sarah: 'Kate, would you like to do the activities in the book and talk to me?'
Kate: [nods as she reads the first page]

Lull (1985) contends that researchers need to develop and maintain good relations with children and family members while also attempting to maintain an objective stance. Jordan (2006:177) claims that to connect with families in social research and to obtain valid and textured images of what their lives are like may require a level of self-disclosure that many social science researchers such as Lull and others would consider problematic. Jordan (2006:170) further argues that in the field researchers are understood and labelled by family members as they attempt to 'construct a role for the researcher and define the situation according to their needs, understandings and experiences'. At first glance the above interaction might appear to be the first stage in the development of good relations between Sarah and Kate. However, what is also taking place is the establishment of common ground between two social actors through shared knowledge of category membership.

Part of what takes place in the interaction above is the co-construction of data (Jordan 2006) where Sarah is a component of the cultural environment that she studies (Denzin 2000; Oakley 1981). Sarah's interaction with Kate illustrates a clear example of a researcher's self-disclosure. It serves a specific purpose, an evident attempt on Sarah's part to connect with Kate and part of the ongoing renegotiation of informed consent. Kate is active in identifying what she needs from Sarah to make sense about why she is being asked to participate and why Sarah is interested. Baker (2003:410) contends that the social order and rationality that participants such as Kate are seeking to ascertain is not imposed in an interview context but 'assembled' by the participants using their 'common sense' member[ship] resources'. In consequence such interviews are displays of 'culture in action' (Hester and Eglin 1997).

As discussed in Chapter 4, gaining informed consent is a dynamic, ongoing and often complex process, that requires us to reflexively consider (Sin 2005) how it is negotiated and re-negotiated in the field. However, the complexity of gaining it and its relationship to category membership and self-disclosure is overlooked in many research texts.

In the account above Kate is seeking information that will help her to either refuse or agree to participate in the interview. Initially Sarah gives some general information about why she wants to talk to Kate but then discloses that she is an adoptive mother with a daughter who was also born in China. It is this information in particular that Kate employs in her next question by asking for more personal information which she then goes on to use in her decision to participate. Holstein and Gubrium (1997:123) argue that during 'active interviewing' the role of the interviewer is to 'incite respondents' answers, virtually activating narrative production...by indicating-even suggesting-narrative positions, resources, orientations and precedents'. In response to Kate's questions Sarah's self-disclosure effectively positions her in the wider canonical and contested narratives about intercountry adoption (Richards 2012b). This positioning as a member of the intercountry adoption community was perhaps taken as an indication to what narratives were wanted and how they might be received. This assembling ensures that both separate individuals, regardless of their adult or child status, become recognised as members of the same group. This common ground establishes the basis for the interview.

Sin (2005:290) argues that in seeking and gaining consent, objectivity and impartiality 'are mere illusions'. If such subtle articulation of membership categorisation is indeed taking place in the early interactions between researcher and respondent then connections are being established during informed consent negotiations which shape the data to come. How these connections are achieved and what impacts they potentially have should be subject to greater interrogation in the wider research community. A further important point to make here is that one participant of this exchange is a nine-year-old girl where it is evident she is using category membership to inform her decision making. This illuminates children's capacity and expertise to engage in research as competent social agents. Kate demonstrates explicit social skills as she gathers the information she needs from Sarah using category membership.

Intercountry adoption as a membership category revealed in the interaction above is picked up later in this chapter but here we want to identify the role and use of self-disclosure as a means to alleviate anxiety about taking part in the research, establish a sense of trust through such disclosure and to allow a rapport between Sarah and Kate to develop. Jordan (2006:173) argues that researchers are studied by respondents for the impressions they 'give' and 'give off' in order to anticipate how the researcher will respond to them and their knowledge. If self-disclosure achieves these elements then it is potentially a very useful (if epistemologically messy) tool and 'strategy' in the research process (Abell et al. 2006:223). Ethnomethodological analyses of interview data are argued to be a far more reflexive research practice than most other approaches. Baker (2003:411) contends that through such analysis it

> becomes impossible not to see the artful practices of interviewer and interviewee in making the interview happen, and consequently it becomes very difficult to unhitch 'answers' from their (em)bedding in an actual, local situation of production

Some researchers claim that self-disclosure can be used to manage and 'counteract' unequal power relations in research relationships (Abell et al. 2006:221). Eder and Fingerson (2003) contend that researchers can empower young respondents by self-disclosure which enables them to share similar experiences. Sarah's self-disclosure clearly facilitated disclosures from Kate. It is argued that when those being studied have a sense that they are understood by someone who faces the same life challenges, a certain level of reciprocity and trust can emerge (see also Oakley 1981). Sarah certainly was not claiming similar life challenges but she did imply a connection through adoption which seemed to influence Kate's decision to take part. Poindexter (2003), like Sin (2005), argues that self-disclosure plays a role in positioning the researcher in the interaction. However, she adds that this should not be 'excessive, gratuitous, or self-serving' (2003:401). Though it is hard to argue that self-disclosure is not self-serving given the ways in which it is articulated in conversation. No one self-discloses to deliberately disadvantage themselves in the social interaction. Saying no to an unknown researcher in your living room may be hard but saying no to a group member is perhaps harder, particularly between adult and child. Sarah may have been seeking to establish a rapport but she used ways to articulate connection and category membership to do this. Did Sarah's self-disclosure make it easier for Kate to consent or harder for her to refuse? These are the dilemmas that come when we acknowledge that the research process is more messy and more agonising than we often admit it to be. Respondents may however, not always interpret the interviewer's behaviour in the intended way. Abell et al. (2006:241) argue that

> through a sharing of experiences the interviewer paradoxically exemplifies differences between themselves and the interviewee in terms of age, gender, social class, race, religion and education. Moreover, such strategies may display an interviewer's greater category entitlement to provide information about a particular topic than the interviewee.

Though underexplored in research studies, self-disclosure can clearly fulfil several functions in research strategies related to informed consent, and building trusting relationships as well as have consequences in interviews. Despite extensive debate and value placed upon objectivity and neutrality, Reinharz (1979) argues that human research should use the researcher as an instrument with tools like personal experiences. These are increasingly becoming recognised as valid sources of scholarly knowledge (Riessman 1994 in Shah 2006:217). Sarah certainly used self-disclosure and category entitlement in gaining respondents for her research and on occasion in the interviews as a way of facilitating discussion. This approach was described by one interviewee as being

> [o]ne mother talking to another who has knowledge of what I am talking about.

The quote above leads the discussion onto the challenges faced by being categorised as an insider in the research context. Initially some of the ethical implications of this status are identified.

## Insider status

Coffey (1999:28) has claimed that the way we conduct our research, the role we take, how we understand and interpret the knowledge we are given is shaped by who we are and the categories we belong to. Griffith (1998) extends this perspective by arguing that who we are is continuously moving between aspects of the researchers biographical profile, the relationship with the community under study and the necessary 'outsideness' of being a researcher.

Sarah's self-disclosure of her status as an intercountry adoptive mother was instrumental in gaining respondents in what is a celebrated and contested field of family formation (Richards 2013). Having gained respondents, her insider status as an intercountry adopter arguably shaped the knowledge she was given and how she understood the stories told. Those championing the role of insiders in social research (see, for example, Leicester 1999; Oakley 1981; Shah 2006; Taylor 2011) claim that 'as a result of social distances, interviewees may not trust researchers, understand questions, or they may purposely mislead their responses' (Miller and Glassner 1997:101) Though insider status may hold some significant advantages (see Montgomery 2007), it also complicates the researcher's role and their membership in the group where they are considered to be the insider (Taylor 2011). While some research approaches clearly find this stance problematic, Coffey (1999:47) argues that these tensions serve to remind us of important ethnographic dichotomies, 'involvement versus detachment', 'distance versus intimacy' and 'stranger versus friend'.

The following account explores the articulation of Sarah's status as a member of the group being studied, and how this shapes the interaction, is explicit:

Angela: 'I explained about the question that people always ask, you know the one... "Is she yours?" I explained to Lisa [her daughter] that "they are not asking if you are my daughter but actually asking if you are adopted". "People do not always know how to use the right words but that's what they mean." I wanted to give her a framework for her about the questions and so I can say to her "do you want Mummy to answer this question? And if so what would you like Mummy to say?" And she said, "yes tell them I am yours and that I am from China", and so I said "ok".'

'You know the one', is said based on Sarah being a member of the category of intercountry adoptive mother. Angela as the interviewee seeks Sarah's acknowledgement to confirm the commonality of intrusive questions about family members. The strategies that the interviewee then goes on to outline in response to intrusive questions are also provided in the context of being between one mother and another where mutual understanding is assumed and displayed. Krieger (1987) contends that such knowledge can produce insight into the topic itself while also illustrating the complexities of positions for the researcher. However, acknowledgement of insider status and category membership on the part of the researcher is initially required along with a critical reflexivity of the ways in which these memberships shape the research. Ristock and Pennell (1996:66) claim that researchers should start their analyses from the personal and indicate the ways in which personal locations and identities inform and shape the research process. However, like self-disclosure, insider status calls into question a researcher's capacity to research the field as others might. Familiar environments are argued to 'produce superficial accounts which fail to penetrate the taken-for-granted relationships that are routine and mundane for the insider' (Howarth 2002:22).

This is contested by researchers such as Leicester (1999), Oakley (1981) and Shah (2006:210) who each claim that 'interviewing individuals with similar experiences encourages the generation of richer material'. Feminist social researchers have provided considerable literature to the debate about the strengths and, indeed, the limitations of researching as a group member or an insider, defined by Thornton (1995) as holding 'subcultural capital' and by Roseneil (1993) as being 'empirically literate'. Many claim that prior knowledge of the group and its members facilitates deeper understanding and a more trusting rapport with participants (Taylor 2011). However, holding insider status represents ethical challenges (Stacey 1996) in the field and unforeseen dilemmas. The following account illustrates some of the ethical complexities of being an insider in the research field.

'I'll do yours if you do mine.'

The above quotation came from a potential respondent in Sarah's research who expressed an interest in taking part with her children. Participants were being recruited through the adoptive organisation which Sarah was also a member of. Sarah asked if her children had any questions about the research and whether they were also interested in taking part. The answer suggested that the children would participate if the mother wanted them to and that, in turn, she would like Sarah to contribute to her own photographic study. Sarah's desire for respondents (she had very few at this point) was strong and refusing such a request from a willing one risked alienating her, particularly problematic given their shared membership of the organisation Children Adopted from China (CACH). However, the children were not (at this point) offering their own consent. Furthermore, Sarah was also being asked to disclose personal information and artefacts that as a mother she perceived not to belong to her but belonged to her daughter to either offer or refuse. Sarah attempted to reduce tensions that come with saying no by suggesting that she had to comply with an ethical framework laid out by the university (which, of course, is true), and that this mother's children were perhaps not ready to offer their consent. In addition, Sarah's own daughter was not yet old enough to make an informed decision about offering the requested material. Sarah suggested that each could get back in touch with the other if things changed. No further contact was made.

Homans (1949 in Plummer 2001) has claimed that methodology is about strategy not morality, but we argue that methodology moves beyond simply a strategy which sets out a moral and ethical position representative of little more than a pattern for 'following the rules' (Plummer 2001:227). It also involves the researcher in making complex, ethical decisions in the moment (Wall 2010) through personal moral perspectives. Such decisions are complicated by category membership relations. Multiple categories were articulated in the above account: researcher, mother and member of CACH all with values and conventions which need to be negotiated while maintaining good relations with another member. Each of these discrete category membership roles are connected, emerging and influencing each other in the research field. Mauthner and Doucet (2003:421) claim that 'the interpersonal, political and institutional contexts in which researchers are embedded' play a key role in shaping their decisions in the field (see also Bell and Newby 1977; Bell and Roberts 1984). How these category memberships shape the role is still underexplored in research publications.

All the examples in this chapter rely on the relevant knowledge that comes with shared category membership and insider status whereby the social actors involved are able to better understand each other. Disagreement remains about whether or not researchers should be members of the groups that they study, despite persuasive claims that subjective knowledge is necessary to appreciate the life experiences of individuals. Maintaining a balance between 'academic credibility' and 'community accountability' can be difficult and induce dilemmas about what to disclose as a researcher and what to omit in the interests of being a member of the group (Taylor 2011:14). Burke (1989 in Taylor 2011) questions whether such use of intimate knowledge can be considered ethical and has described this stance as 'privileged eavesdropping'. Others more simply claim that researchers need to be skilled in maintaining the boundary of being both researcher and insider (Taylor 2011).

What is evident is that insiderness and category membership induce ethical dilemmas which all but the most reflexive ethnographic accounts exclude from discussions (Madden 2010). Situating ourselves both socially and emotionally in relation to our respondents is an important element of the reflexive process (Mauthner and Doucet 2003:419). However, it is too simplistic to identify categories such as gender, sexuality, class or even family formation and imply understanding, commonality or shared values as a result of these categories. Howarth (2002:23) claims that an assumption that 'common social identification produces shared knowledge and experiences' is 'patronising and essentialistic'. The account above, whereby Sarah was asked to reciprocate research participation, revealed greater differences between researcher and participant than shared values or experiences, but the interaction was premised on an assumption of insider status between fellow members of the same small group of individuals. In this instance for the researcher, a category of insider status made consent negotiations more problematic where discussions not only involved the research activity but ongoing membership relations in a shared group. Research has shown what Taylor (2011:13) describes as 'rules of engagement'. Belonging to specific groups and holding insider status also has rules, and the two are not necessarily compatible. This makes 'role displacement and confusion' (ibid.) important aspects of these relationships, which should at the very least be identified and explored for their ethical implications. Ultimately, researchers 'can only strive to be intellectually poised between familiarity and strangeness' (Hammersley and Atkinson 1995:112). But without more research-based interrogation of how familiarity and difference are constructed and used in interviews and subsequent data analysis, little can be gained beyond a token acknowledgement that familiarity has to be managed.

Baker (2003:401) claims that '[i]nterviews are definitely not "time out" from the social worlds that the participants are talking about; rather, they are reflexive descriptions of those worlds'. This challenges the perception that interviews are 'self-contained events' (Phoenix 2008:71). Therefore, the identity attributes and category memberships we embody in everyday life also shape the interview and data creation process. Too often, identity categories are initially and sometimes tokenistically identified but then overlooked as influences in the analyses or interpretative process. We suggest that our respective multiple category memberships should be made explicit, making it possible to discuss how these intersect with the respondents when analysing data (Patai 1991:149).

Using category membership to identify potential respondents and then constructing category membership during interviews are important steps to successfully establish an entitlement to speak authoritatively about a topic (Phoenix 2008). It is this category entitlement that we explore next.

## Category entitlement

People construct identities through telling their stories and life experiences. These descriptions construct and reveal the category memberships of the tellers. Through category membership, entitlement to speak authoritatively about a subject is established (Phoenix 2008; Potter 1996). This entitlement is not static but can be constructed or eroded within discourse (Potter 1996).

Sarah claimed her entitlement to discuss intercountry adoption from China by stating her membership of the intercountry adoption group from where her participants were drawn. For example, she verbally reinforced this entitlement in the discussion with Kate by stating that she was an adoptive mother. Similarly, Allison revealed her own membership to the 'parent's of disabled children's club' when she swapped stories with Paul, a teacher whose daughter was also an Augmentative and Alternative Communications Systems user. Allison reflected on how this revelation forged an unspoken bond between them, and they each gave a silent 'nod' to the others entitlement to this exclusive, members-only club. Mandelbaum (1978) contends that stories and accounts are collaboratively constructed. This perspective is evident in the previous account where Angela confirmed Sarah's entitlement to discuss intrusive family questions through identifying the typical question that many parents of transracially adopted children are asked, stating 'you know the one'. Potter (1996) argues that category entitlement removes the necessity to question how a person has acquired topic knowledge. Group membership is deemed as sufficient legitimacy for holding knowledge of a specific topic or domain. Through affirming this mutual 'insider' experience between researcher and respondent, entitlement is reaffirmed and the rapport between researcher and respondent can be strengthened (Abell et al. 2006). This arguably increases the trust and potentially encourages the respondent to speak more openly and may encourage the researcher to reciprocate through self-disclosure. Both participants in the discourse build this category membership and subsequent entitlement, and both are consequently committed and invested in the discussion.

Phoenix (2008; see also Sacks 1974) argues that social actors construct their entitlement through revealing related experiences and how they position themselves in relation to the topic. However, she also argues that assumptions about entitlement can occur. The following account is taken from Sarah's research and reveals shared knowledge, but not comfortable rapport between interviewee and interviewer. Here Linda shares her experiences of receiving a referral for adoption from China. This documentation included a photograph of the baby she had been matched with.

Linda: 'What arrived was the most unattractive photograph of a funny little thing with hair sticking up obviously taken when she was much younger than the paperwork suggested. Just for a few minutes, I was disappointed. I think that I had this fantasy picture in my mind, and it was not realised in the picture in front of me and then I asked myself, "well what do you want, a fantasy, pretty child or do you want to give a real child with nothing a home?" And as soon as I thought that it was fine and I wouldn't have cared if she had turned out to be plain. It was the same with my second daughter too. I saw her picture and thought Urgh! But then you think, this is a child that nobody wants and the minute I thought that it was fine. I guess the order of what I wanted them to be like was firstly good natured, then clever and then to have looks, but I would have accepted anything really.'

During interviews, interviewees can tell their stories and experiences without knowing how the researcher may receive them but mutual category membership provides clues about the type of stories expected and accepted (Phoenix 2008). In this narrative, Linda admits to feelings and aspirations in motherhood that are not usual for mothers to express, even if they may be very common. Her account contrasts with what is culturally acceptable to say. However, as a member of an intercountry adoptive category Linda perhaps feels entitled to reveal her feelings and can do so with an authority of knowledge and behaviour within this group. Linda's entitlement to share these experiences with Sarah is therefore based on their shared category membership. Sarah's complicit understanding of these non-normative statements on Linda's part is both imagined and assumed, while for Sarah, the desire to gather Linda's stories, and remain in good relations with this fellow member, mutes how she might have otherwise responded. Shah (2006:211) reminds us of the dangers of 'over-rapport' when we research a topic where we hold what Stanley and Wise (1993:227–228) call 'Epistemological privilege'. Linda's statements reinforced the need for Sarah to follow advice given by (Bondi 2003 in Shah 2006:211) of remaining 'emotionally present and reactive to the interviewees' responses' as well as reflecting on her own feelings. Category entitlement dictates that people are treated as knowledgeable in certain contexts. Yet, assumptions about what one is entitled to say and how it will be received on the basis of membership do occur, and being a member it is not necessarily straightforward (Widdicombe and Woofitt 1995). Furthermore, people can fail to be treated as members, and some categories are negotiable (Jayyusi 1984) where entitlement is either built up through the interaction or undermined, as in the examples explored below.

Particular life experiences of children are frequently the reason for their participation in research. As Uprichard (2010) has previously argued, children do not participate in the way that adults do in research generally but are included by virtue of their status as school pupil, family member, young carer and so on. Categories attributed to children, such as pupil, adoptee or disabled, categorise children prior to and outside the normative category of childhood and arguably serve to marginalise and exclude the very children we seek to include in our research discussions. Their membership of a particular category such as these is commonly the prerequisite for taking part. In some cases, this membership not only predicates specific knowledge and entitlements but carries a variety of traits, characteristics and behavioural expectations (see Chapter 6 for further discussion of adoptee attributes). Sacks (1974) refers to these as 'category-bound' activities associated with membership. For example, in Sarah's research young adoptees were expected to be engaged in specific culture-related activities to ensure that their Chinese heritage was accessible to them. Some of the young participants spoke at length about attending Chinese summer school, having Mandarin classes, visiting China and being a member of CACH. However Finch (1984) has argued that interviewers should not assume commonalities. Category membership for children may not be something that they have constructed themselves but can be a status attributed to them (Drew 1978) by adults in general or researchers in particular. Assumptions about which categories individuals wish to claim can also occur. Sarah found this particularly so with the adoptees in her research. The parents interviewed did not challenge the category of adoptive parent as the primary reason for being interviewed and positioned themselves as being entitled to talk authoritatively within this category. But as Hacking (1986) reminds us, such truths and realities can be resisted.

A number of older girls (aged between 9 and 12 years) emphasised other categories that they claimed membership to during the interviews and, on occasion, actively sought to distance themselves and undermine their membership of an adoptive category. Some girls constructed category membership of 'best friend' or 'pupil' as indicated below:

Kate (nine years): 'I like to hang out with my friends and go shopping. I like to go swimming club and football club. I like to do sporty things. I like to put on mini shows. I like going to my gang show rehearsals.'

Louise (nine years): 'My special friend is Sasha because she is my best friend and very nice. We like hanging out and chasing and annoying the boys.'

Jenny (aged 12 years) refused to acknowledge her membership of adoptive category by remaining silent about her adoption and also, on occasion, by challenging her mother about the obligatory nature of the Chinese culture related activities that her membership in this category and family demanded. In contrast, she was eloquent in her aspirations to visit New York, to own a pet, about socialising with friends and taking part in school activities.

Jenny: 'School is fun because all of us – my friends all go round in a big group talking, playing and laughing.'

In Mel's (aged 12 years) statement below, she resists the category through which she is being asked to speak:

Mel: 'I am more than just adopted; I don't feel like I am different to everyone else just because I was adopted.'

These responses are part of a wider social construction of adoption, and what is evident are the ways in which these young girls construct their category memberships just as adults do. The girls here also demonstrate the capacity to develop their identities by both establishing and resisting category entitlement. This occurs even within adult/child power relations where parents and researchers assume an emphasis on a category membership that the girls themselves do not wish to give such prominence. As social actors, this negotiation demonstrates a level of relational agency and autonomy that is rarely attributed to children.

## Conclusion

Our individual category memberships (both those we claim and those attributed to us) shape who we are, who we can be and how we perceive and are perceived in our social worlds. These memberships influence our interactions and inform not only what we think and say but what others anticipate we may think and say.

Our data cannot be extracted from this 'complex web of intimate and larger social relations' (Mauthner and Doucet 2003:422). Our 'scientific stories' (Haraway 1991:106) therefore are not blank slates, they are constructed through specific locations and interdependent social relationships which in turn are informed by our category memberships.

Such memberships extend far beyond fundamental and more obvious categories such as gender, sexuality or ethnicity. This can make reflexive consideration of their influence a complex, rather messy and, at times almost self-indulgent affair which may not reflect the requirements of funders or institution (see Chapter 1). However where we situate ourselves and our respondents, influences what we ask, how we ask, and the responses we get. Categories establish our entitlement to speak; they also shape what we can say and how our voices will be interpreted. Voices thus become heard through the categories that we as individuals claim or that we have been attributed to. Our voices are thus understood through the categories held or claimed by those who listen. Acknowledging that establishing category membership and constructing category entitlement in fieldwork is taking place, it is a neglected and important ethical position for each of us to take as we seek to analyse the 'self-reflective accounts' (Mauthner and Doucet 2003) we collect.

# 6
# Privileging Voices

## Introduction

It has already been established that the social studies of childhood regard children's voices as credible and worthy of being listened to. Indeed, James and Prout (1997) go as far as to suggest that the inclusion of their voices is a matter of need and right. As a consequence, the drive to give children a voice, to make their voices heard and understood is well documented in academic literature. However, Lewis (2008:14) describes the search for children's voices as a 'powerful moral crusade', and she argues that since this quest has gathered such a pace, it has persuaded researchers that innovative means of gathering voices produce data that is authentic, realistic and representative of all children. She goes on to suggest that its assumed relationship with truth and experience has privileged the concept of voice in qualitative enquiry. We agree with this sentiment and also believe that this approach does little to engage critically with methodological and epistemological limits of voice. Even as self-confessed gatherers of children's voices, we have come to question the ethical positions of those who claim to represent others' voices; who interpret personal accounts; and who sort and sieve data. Through undertaking research of our own, we have come to understand that it is within these very processes that conventional voices and those that are the most easily heard and understood are privileged, and those whose voices are harder to seek and to hear remain marginalised.

The discussions in this chapter will illuminate the ways in which some voices are heard and documented more than others. While we draw predominantly on Allison's research with disabled children and young people, we consider that the key issues we raise relate to many children whose voices remain unheard. We contend that children's influence in research, policies and service practice has been negligible, and we argue that complex debates relating to competency, age and maturity and the credibility of their statements are the main causes for this. Some studies are adultist and thereby rely heavily on data collected from parents and professionals. We therefore suggest that marginalised children and young people's voices tend to be overwritten by adults who talk at them, about them and on their behalf. We suggest that as a consequence, the resulting silence is neither neutral nor empty. It supports the ascribed collective identity of passivity, vulnerability and dependency. This not only affects children's social status in general but continues to support the cultural schema and collective understanding of childhoods.

Including children with unconventional voices often presents researchers with significant challenges and facilitating their inclusion requires a considerable investment in time, resources and the development of new skills. In addition, it also calls for adaptations to research designs and methodologies. However, the exclusions of populations based on assumptions of vulnerability, incapacity or incompetence is highly problematic. It is no longer acceptable to exclude voices simply because they are considered incompetent or pose challenges to traditional research methods. Therefore, recognition of strength-based perceptions of children, who are regarded as experts in their own lives (James and Prout 1997), as active citizens with participation rights (UNCRC 1989) and within principles of ethical symmetry (Christensen and Prout 2002) are central to the discussions in this chapter.

Conventional meanings of 'voice' assume naturally produced speech as a means of expression. Here a question arises: Are unconventional voices heard in the same way, or does having a different voice implicate participation? The following discussions will explore the concept of voice and examine the types of voices that we choose to (or are able to) listen to. The ways in which some voices are privileged will also be examined. We will use our collective narratives to illustrate how the taken-for-granted general disposition and collective identity of children and childhood is influenced by what Bourdieu terms the 'doxa' (1977:167) – the universe of the undiscussed and undisputed.

This chapter sets out to examine the choices we make about the voices we listen to, how we listen to them and why we consider some to be more authentic than others. It builds resistance to what has become the comfortable and accepted positioning and constitution of 'voice'.

## Silences and inventions

Some research decisions affect whose stories get told and which voices get used. Some voices inevitably get lost. While not disputing that 'listening to children's voices' should be embedded in and at the forefront of ethical principles, we question whether liminal voices are sufficiently captured for we believe that we naturally gravitate towards those that are the most recognised and easy to hear.

Allison's research with children who have little or no speech enabled her to spend much time with the young participants, getting to know them and them to know her as they worked and played together in school. As the fieldwork progressed and they became more familiar, the entries from her reflective journal illustrated the pen pictures that she had begun to draw of each participant. The memo's she scribbled in the margins of the observations mostly related to their cognitive ability and communication skills. On reflection, the entries also demonstrated that she had inadvertently started to 'grade individuals' (Watson 2003:36), privileging some voices and gravitating more towards the children and young people who were easier to communicate with. This effectively attributed them with higher status. For example, one of the young participants often declined to communicate with her directly. He chose instead to look away or hang his head. After several failed attempts, the conversations became less frequent and Allison interpreted his silence as an inability to communicate. As a consequence, this submergence of voice stigmatised him as 'other' and she ascribed his social status as such. However, a research conversation with a member of staff who had many years of experience of working with this young man enlightened her:

> If Jorge doesn't want to communicate, he won't communicate with you either verbally, facially or using the machine. It's just a case of 'I'm not talking today'. He has a lot of complex physical needs, but if he could walk away sometimes, I'm sure he would.

Allison reflected on her assumptions. She concluded that not only were her interpretations outrageously judgmental, they were quite wrong. While Jorge could quite easily understand her and was perfectly capable of communicating with her, he had simply chosen not to. Similarly, Paterson and Hughes (1999) concluded that people with communication difficulties are often ignored and made to feel inferior due to their inability to communicate according to societally defined norms of accepted speech. With this now at the forefront of her thinking, she realised that she should have respected his silences as equally as his spoken narratives and paid heed to the advice given by Agar (1980) who advocates that ethnographers should realise that when a person withholds their opinion, it does not necessarily mean that they do not have one. She felt that she has also done what Crapanzano described as 'marking boundaries' (1986:52) and used both space and silence to invent her own construction of his identity, framing his dependency in what Hockey and James refer to as 'the metaphoric role of childhood' (1993:10). This clearly reflects Bourdieu's notion of habitus which represents the social worlds of actors: 'the relationship between two capacities define the habitus, the capacity to produce classifiable practices and worlds, and the capacity to differentiate and appreciate those practices and products' (1986a:17). Allison's observations provided static definitions and based on this, she judged that this young participant was unable to communicate, placing him in a defining and deterministic category of 'hard to reach' and 'unresponsive'. While Edwards and Imrie (2003) suggest that reactions such as these may often be unthinking and spontaneous, they warn that they can also be as a result of being unconsciously learned.

Emerging from this scenario is what Bourdieu (1977:79) suggests is unconscious behaviour, closely related to habit and habituation whereby actions become taken for granted and undisputed. Jorge's practice of silence and his ability to 'withhold access to his world' (Mandell 1991:37) was clearly not appreciated. Because he had chosen not to interact, he was a clean slate on which Allison was able to write her own view of who he was and what he was able to do. The misjudgement denied his competency and she perceived him incapable of achieving specific outcomes. This, she reflected, could have ultimately excluded him from the research project and his voice, like many others before him, would have been lost. In addition, Jorge may have experienced this abject identification on previous occasions and, as a result, decided not to participate in any form of further conversation. Indeed, as Gilligan (1993) warns, the relational identities borne out of taken-for-granted attitudes can become a self-fulfilling prophecy and responses often follow as a matter of course. Clearly, this young man was prepared to allow the ventriloquised representation of him to remain unchallenged and, as a consequence, Allison's (mis)interpretation assigned him to a pre-ordained habitus, categorising him by impairment. Jessica's experience of supervising a student through a series of ethical approval processes highlights that it is not just disabled children and young people who must deal with being identified or labelled as incompetent or unable to participate. The language of assent discussed in Chapter 1 assumes a level of incompetency of all children whereby they are perceived as being unable to understand the requirements of social interactions or research relationships. These constructions serve to position them as structurally vulnerable. However, in Allison's example of Jorge, discussed above, there is also evidence of this young person's ability to negotiate competently adults' expectations of him. Jorge uses silence here as a demonstration of his power, it is a mechanism of resistance. The staff in the setting state he would walk away if he could, in Jorge's case he cannot but he can and does remove his voice. This demonstrates use of silence in a different way, as resistance and if we don't realise how children (and adults) use their voices in these ways then we are not really listening.

The general dispositions of disabled children and young people are often based on the overriding ascribed collective identity, 'disabled' or to put it another way, a taken-for-granted collective identity which is often understood as a consequence of medical classification. As language is a central aspect of the study of identity that affects and dominates identity construction (Strauss 1977), Allison had based this young person's behaviour on stereotypical criteria associate with 'disability' and categorised him as passive and dependent. While projecting negative assumptions such as these, she had denied difference, diversity and voice. She had privileged some participant's voices and subjugated others and done just as Fawcett (2000) suggests, accepted social constructions and categories that tend to reflect dominant and social groupings.

Further familiarisation visits however, helped Allison to gain a greater understanding of Jorge's personalised method of communication. Spending more time with him in the classroom enabled her to get to know him better and as they built up mutual trust, he chose to become more communicative. While critical self-reflections such as these enabled her to form a nuanced understanding of the general dispositions of disabled children and young people, they also enabled her to move beyond the general to the specific and revise her understanding of the diversities of individual childhoods.

The scenario has been used to illustrate the ways in which disabled children and young people's identities are based on accepted perceptions and cultural schemas of disability, all of which are, using Bourdieu's terms of reference, embedded in 'methodologies for adapting generalised knowledge to a range of particular practices in particular locations in time and space' (1977:78–79). However, we were curious to know *how* this process privileges some voices over others. We concluded that if some children and young people are not able to communicate in conventional ways, they may feel disadvantaged in their ability to contribute to research conversations. They may also feel that their contributions are devalued. In addition, and as the example suggests, the severely limited feedback from Jorge allowed space for invention free from correction. Clearly, silences can easily be filled by others who speak on behalf of those whose absence of conventional modes of movement, speech or verbal communication renders them 'speech-less'. Indeed, as Edwards and Imrie (2003) suggest, some voices then simply disappear. Acts that constitute relations of hierarchy and power often lead to withdrawal of voice and without recourse, silence ensues. Arguably, within this silence, identities can be misunderstood, misinterpreted or simply invented by those whose voices are louder, more powerful. As a consequence, some voices are privileged and some are silenced.

## Influences that position children's voices

While there has been an increase in policy priority to include children and young people in decision making in general, Franklin and Sloper (2009) found that very little is known about specific factors that promote disabled children's participation. Arguably, without providing opportunities, platforms for voice or providing optimal conditions that make the recursive activity of listening to children's voices a reality, limited examples of empirical research, especially with those who have learning difficulties or severe communication impairments, will continue and external structures that mark disabled children as vulnerable and incompetent will persist.

## Images of dependency

Shakespeare (2000) contends that while disability continues to be represented by images of dependency, the dominant and positive imagery that surrounds helpers in our society portrays workers in the caring profession as highly valued and respected. He goes on to suggest that the establishment of expertise and power of helpers serves not only to privilege their voices, but also to ensure their superior status whereas the service users' voices 'remain silenced, objectified and othered, in a discourse where they exist only to have things done to them or for them' (Shakespeare 2000:21). He went on to pursue this point further by examining pre-existing ideas of the cultural representation of disability and dependency. He argued that 'normal' bodies are legitimised and those with 'in-valid' or 'deviant' bodies are seen to be inferior or in need of help. While we believe that the concept of representation can clearly be applied to children with unconventional voices, once again we draw on Allison's empirical research to help justify this claim. She observed that some of the young participants needed help to access their Augmentative and Alternative Communication Systems (AACS). Her field notes highlighted that the inaccessibility of some AACS limited the opportunities of use and this, she believed, excluded their voices. For example, one young participant's device was kept in a *'rucksack on the handlebars of her wheelchair'*. She could not access the bag that contained it without help. In addition, she could not open the bag and take the AACS out without support and she also needed help to set her AACS on the tray of her wheelchair. Her use of it was totally governed by her 'able-bodied' adult helper. A conversation with another young participant, Cherise revealed that she had to rely on adults help to set the device up for her as she did not have fine motor skills strong enough to undo the Velcro fastenings of the bag that housed it. She also had to ask for help if the battery needed recharging. She explained that as a wheelchair user, she could not access the electric plug sockets that were positioned at floor level in most classrooms. Allison concluded that both participants were clearly disabled by their environment and there were many barriers that served to exclude their voices. This example clearly strengthens our argument: voices that are easily heard and within reach typically become privileged. The stories told here support the argument for a less polarised, more interactional approach towards including children in research. It also suggests that without including marginalised voices, we will continue to assume the collective identity of children and therefore the homogenisation of childhood.

### Borrowed voices

The majority of the children in Allison's study relied on others to programme their communication aids, so if any new vocabulary was needed, the staff would take the device away for a few hours to input specific words. One of the young participant's readily demonstrated the comprehensive dash-board bank of pre-programmed words and phrases that she had on her AACS that she used to communicate. She also told Allison that she 'often typed her words herself'. Allison observed that most of the pre-programmed vocabulary on the young people's AACS's related to curriculum subjects and she felt that this impacted on the study, for the research conversations relied heavily on words lent to them by adults. On reflection, this made the authenticity of voice questionable. Issues of access to and maintenance of the AACS's, together with the limited choice of words available to the participants clearly influenced the young participants' voices. Just as in Sarah and Jess's research, Allison concluded that the voices of the young people were very much governed by the adult practices and attitudes. Indeed, this demonstrates that those with 'normal' or 'conventional' voices were legitimised and those with 'in-valid' or 'deviant' voices were seen as inferior and in need of help. As a consequence, the children and young people with little or no speech became reliant on others with conventional speech to provide them access to a voice or alternatively, to speak on their behalf.

## The symbolic representation of voice

Those with very little speech and others literally without voice are often offered prosthetics in the form of high-tech communication aids in order to secure the right to speak for themselves and make decisions and choices about their lived experiences. While on the one hand, such prosthetics can be seen as empowering and a means of giving them a voice, on the other, they can be seen to act as systems of symbolic representation that lead to oppressive practices. Indeed, in Allison's study, the analysis of the data revealed that in some instances, the children's specific position practices in terms of their levels of cognitive and physical ability were represented by the specific type of AACS they used. During a research conversation, one of the members of the teaching staff told Allison about a young AACS user who had recently been given a new aid:

> He's recently got a new one, um, one with much higher specs than he needs and we were interested to see if he would take it on board intellectually. He had new pages he needed to remember and recall. He has a lot more pages in this machine and he has surprised us 'cos he is gaining knowledge all the time which is really good.

During another conversation, a member of staff compared one user with another:

> Stuart can be very able on his machine but he's not as at home with it as Jack, he needs much more guidance as to what page he will find something on ... if you can't find it, Stuart can't find it ... you need to push him.

On more than one occasion, the data illustrated that adults' perceptions of the disabled children and young people's position practices were interpreted and based on their use of high-tech communication aids. The AACS represented the symbolic value of the children's cognitive foundations of status which, in turn, created hierarchies of social location within the classroom. This indicated that some of the staff believed that the type of aid allocated to each participant reflected their identity. For example, the more functions the aid had, the higher the user's cognitive ability was assumed to be:

> When someone is cognitively more able, they [the aids] are fantastic and they can use them really, really well.

The smaller the aid, the less physically difficulties the user has:

> They are small, that's the problem for the variety and volume of vocabulary the buttons get smaller and smaller and smaller, um, so those with more profound physical difficulties or those with visual impairments can't use the more powerful machines

And, finally, the newer and more personalised the aid, the less likely the user was dependent on external funding:

> That new system is about £4,000 if it can connect onto the original 'tell us' which is what she's got or £11,000 for the new 'tell me' – Lizzie has a trust fund that might fund certain things for her and so her mum has to go and ask the trust if they would like to resource it – if not, its fairly unlikely she will get it.

The conversations with the staff about the AACS used by each participant not only categorised them but were based on what Cunningham explains as 'the basic stock of knowledge that people carry around in their heads as a result of living in particular cultures or subcultures' (1993:1). Identifying the participating disabled children and young people, some AACS determined the users' cognitive ability, others gauged the users' physical impairment and others calculated their financial status. As Bourdieu (1986b) explained, social identity tends to be defined and interpreted through difference. He also argued that groups attribute cultural capital to particular behaviours and they vie to impose their definition of which social phenomena constitute legitimate behaviour on others. The above discussions suggest that the normative expectations and social identities of the young participants were interpreted from fixed unyielding notions based on past relationships or from knowledge inherited from others and the justification of the definitions provided a rationale for behaviour.

Such assumptions based on prior knowledge are not restricted to Allison's respondents but occurs throughout childhood. In Sarah's research it became apparent that ideas about what an orphan is, or should be, informed literature, social work practice and the kinship work done by families. At various points in the research Sarah found some of the following ideas articulated by RECS, social work professionals, adoptive parents and in academic literature. Such knowledge, accurate or otherwise is therefore productive. As Sarah writes in her thesis:

Orphans are claimed to play a pivotal role not only in social welfare provision but in mythology too (Ennew 2005). Orphaned girls in particular, have been a recurring feature of fiction. As characters they are commonly depicted as protagonists (Friedlander 2003) yet vulnerable, loveable objects of charity, the 'tropes of victim hood' (Anzil 2013; Leinaweaver 2008:71). As victims, they are also available to be rescued and hold the key to transforming the lives of those who do the rescuing (Walkerdine 1999:15). In classic and contemporary literature, the orphan is often depicted as someone with a blank canvas upon which identity traits can be inscribed. Collier (2006) argues that through assimilation and appropriation an orphan can be ascribed an identity in the image of her new society and parents, suggesting that a form of colonisation takes place. Walkerdine (1999:15) provides some fictional examples of this perspective, including the story of Annie, who is depicted as a working class, homeless orphan. Despite this destitute and impoverished beginning, she is 'a figure of immense transformative power'. Her fictional role is to use an endearing personality to soften the heart of the adults around her and in so doing, secure a place in a wealthy family. Saunders (2008:1553) argues that a 'defining hallmark' of such literature is the presence of sentimentality, where sympathy for the plight of the character is evident and required from the audience.

Despite Ennew's (2005) argument that there is no global definition for 'orphan', the term does represent extensively held and at times contradictory ideas of the becoming child, of powerlessness, of victim and also, conversely, of being lucky (Emond 2009). The absence, or inclusion of a partial narrative of belonging which each of these children's orphaned status represents, lacks normative connections through family, biography and culture and is considered to be socially problematic. In addition Moeller (1998) argues that the image of orphan is a seductive one and, as with other representations, is effective in undermining the realities of the lives of these children. The role of orphan performs a necessary identity role in the social construction of childhood. This image is argued to evoke pity, sympathy and support (Holland

1992:148). Such a role depicts an 'other' childhood separate to normative childhood which is identified as being embedded in a biological family. Connolly (2000:174) argues that all children are normatively socialised into 'pre-existing racial and gender identities that have been set for them'. Collier (2006) suggests that orphaned children are compelled to play a specific identity role in their adoptive families, offering adoptive parents an opportunity to perform a nurturing protective and loving role. The adopted child then allows the parent to perform and display a version of the family. The orphan's membership in this family is argued to be contingent upon them being willing to comply with the associated obligation and responsibilities and maintain the social order (Bluebond-Langner 1978). However, I contend that all children provide parents similar opportunities and their place in the family carries similar responsibilities. Such opportunities and responsibilities are common to both adopted and biological children.

The orphan as a category upon which identity characteristics may be ascribed has been explored in previous research (see Dorow 2006). Gailey (2000:303) has previously claimed that racial stereotypes of Asian women being 'compliant and docile' inform adopters motives for adoption from China. Such is the linguistic power of terms like orphan and abandoned, Chinese orphan girls, prior to their adoption already have identity characteristics inscribed on them. Some are unique and specific to girls but other traits are assumed to be part of the adoptee's identity through other equally iconic linguistic imagery such as neglect, deprivation and foreign orphanage. Such labels create images which Fraser et al. (2004:39) argue reflect the power of adults to place individual children into depersonalising categories 'that spotlight membership of abnormal categories ahead of membership of childhood'. The language also conveys particular attitudes of behaviour towards certain groups of children (ibid.). A variety of attributes have been linked to an adoptee identity (Bartholet 1999; Jacobson 2008). These are often informed by psychological research. An 'adopted child syndrome' (Kirschner 1990:3) identifies adoptee traits which include attachment disorder, learning disabilities, stealing, lying, violent behaviour, and even setting fires (Jacobson 2008). These attributes are argued to be more prevalent in transracial adoptees (Bartholet 1999). Whilst Kirschner's claim about a syndrome has been robustly challenged (see Friedlander 2003), the notion that adopted children may have particular disorders by virtue of their orphan/adoptee status is taken as self evident. Examples of parents and a professional social worker identifying such traits prior and post adoption are also found in my research. 'Myths and stereotypes' about adoption are prevalent in popular culture (Friedlander 2003:747) and shape how adoption is framed.

Yet, just as Lizzie demonstrates, a perspective which suggests that children are simply the products of such ascription is insufficient. Children can and do play an active role in shaping their identities (Wall 2010), and once recognised, the social context where they negotiate their subject positions must be accounted for (Connolly 2000). One of the most common ways that the girls in Sarah's research resisted such categories was to make statements such as the following:

'I don't feel any different just because I was adopted.'

. . .

'I am more than just adopted.'

Despite the power in these statements and evident attempts to move beyond the category of adoption or adopted, the voices of actual children can be muted by the identity traits placed on their shoulders which they are to a certain extent compelled to perform within their social specific contexts.

In relation to the systems in situ that categorise individuals, Giddens suggests that bodily appearances relating to 'all those features of the surface of the body including modes of dress and adornment, which are visible to the individual and to other agents, and which are ordinarily used as cues to interpret actions' (1991a:99) have relevance to the trajectory of self, particularly in relation to the ways in which bodies reflect social positioning. Clearly, the extracts taken from Allison's data demonstrate how the adults used voice prosthetics as symbolic representations of disabled children and young people's identities. Indeed, Goffman refers to 'props' or 'sign-equipment' (1959:39) as representations of social positioning and suggests that they can be used to reaffirm expressive bias which eventually become accepted as reality. However, Allison concluded that where AACS were used to categorise and identify disabled children and young people, it not only constrained specific aspects of the self but also governed responses of individuals, situating them in social conventions that assume vulnerability and dependency.

The discussions demonstrate how social identities of both 'difference' and 'similarity' are used to categorise children and young people, grouping them together homogenously according to the central values of society. However, while this is useful in terms of understanding their general dispositions, it is vital that their own views are included, for we argue that the general habitus of children and childhood does not reconcile other dimensions of their identity, nor does it account for the ways in which they have forged their own cultures through acts of resistance. It does, however explain why some voices are marginalised and others are privileged.

## Powerful voices

While social practices and the recursiveness of social life tend to settle into what Bourdieu (1986a) terms as habitus which represents the social worlds of actors, we would argue that membership of social worlds and everyday institutional situations is not wholly determined. Uncertainties of membership relate to intricacies of the location and dislocation of multiple identities and disregards individual agency. Arguably, language also regulates human interaction and positions people socially. As 'all human interaction involves the communication of meaning, the operation of power, and modes of normative sanctioning' (Giddens 1991b:46–47), it follows then that actors draw upon specific rules embedded in language to reproduce corresponding structural properties of specific social systems.

The following conversations taken from Allison's study illustrate the ways in which memberships are bounded by institutional orders. For example, a member of staff who had known some of the Sixth Form pupils since they joined the school Nursery, described one of the young participants as 'backward and very passive' and another as 'all singing and dancing'. Another member of staff referred to one of the young participants as 'less able' and another as a 'very complex case'. The point raised here highlights the ways in which voices and competencies are constructed through language. It is also useful to note Bourdieu's (1977) expansion of the notion of habitus to speaking. He refers to the use of symbolic power embedded in the language used by dominated speakers in order to encompass the sense of value to what one has to say in a particular situation. The examples above demonstrated the ways in which the competencies of children were clearly suspended and shaped by dominant adult's voices. As a result, it was adults who made decisions on behalf of the children. The disabled children and young people became what Christensen (1999) termed as muted actors and, by design, the 'helpers' became more powerful and the 'helpless' more needy, less autonomous and less capable.

At this point, it is useful to consider the factors that stabilise expected everyday social functions that are embedded within the examples given in this chapter. We need to critically examine how these influence the participants' voices. The examples authorise properties of the social practice of communication in school whereby adult's voices are privileged. Adults talk, children listen, joining in only when invited, following conventions of social exchange. The children are clearly reluctant to try out the suggested new practices that encourage destabilisation of the ingrained social practices of said membership. While Giddens (1979) believes in actors' competent knowledgeability of their everyday world and recognises that reflexive monitoring of action can reconstitute the (re)organisation of society, an interesting lacuna in this analysis of reflexivity is highlighted. On this occasion, the young participants chose not to initiate conversations or indeed use their discursive consciousness to alter their general dispositions. While this was puzzling, it was not surprising because as has already established, the disabled children and young people's lives were controlled daily by adults in that they were told where, when and how to use their AACS's. Even the words available to them were programmed for them by adults. Borrowing the phrase used by Giddens 'power is always exercised over someone' (1979:341), this suggests that the membership of competency has been ascribed for so long by adults that the set of normative rules of conduct for disabled children are deeply engrained in their daily behaviour. As a consequence, the disabled children's voices have been subordinated to a point where they have become passive and quiet.

Invitations to give voice are unexpected and the call for voice raises anxiety. Indeed, if disabled children and young people are to be empowered to gain competence and confidence, it must be worked at discursively, socially and politically.

## 'Seeing things differently': Privileging children's voices

The discussions so far have focused on the ways in which attitudes and practices influence the general disposition of children and young people. Placing children and young people in hierarchies according to what they can and cannot do effectively privileges some voices over others and the voices that are hard to hear often become silenced. However, in order to gain a more holistic understanding of children's lives and lived childhoods, we believe that their stories should be prioritised and their competence as social actors recognised. The contours and shapes of children's voices are therefore now needed to contextualise the discussions further and so it is time to move the discussion on and include the voices that are hard to hear. An example of the ways in which a young person with little or no natural speech made himself understood becomes clear in the retelling of one incident that occurred during one of Allison's familiarisation visits. She joined a French class where the teacher was telling the class that their task was to translate a letter from Bruno, a French boy, and compose a reply. As the teacher spoke, Leon yawned loudly and used his AACS to type 'boring'. He glanced at Allison, and surreptitiously tilted the aid so that only she could read it. The aid was switched to silent mode. She gestured that she had read the message by raising her eyebrows. The teacher looked over and asked Leon if everything was alright. He smiled and confirmed that it was and quickly erased the message. When the teacher started to talk again, he typed another message: 'we did this before...' and yawned loudly once more. Again, he erased the message quickly while the teacher glanced at him, frowning. Once assigned the task, the young man engaged fully on it until his classmate nudged him and then purposely pushed his bag off the table and onto the floor. Leon was not able to retrieve the bag without help. He was obviously agitated by the incident and used his AACS to tell his neighbour to 'Piss Off!'. This time he turned the volume up and so the whole class heard what he said. The teacher ignored the fracas but walked behind him and picked up the bag. She put it on the table told him to erase the message and indicated that both should get on with their work and stop squabbling. While the dynamics of interactions at work here are undoubtedly complex and open to interpretation, the above observation can be usefully employed to analyse the notion that disability should not be based purely on others' knowledge and opinion. While Allison found that the majority of the staff were concerned that the disabled children and young people were passive in terms of initiating conversations and expressing their needs and desires, the above scenario clearly contradicts this. While we consider that multi-voiced accounts are important to gain a balanced view of childhoods, we argue that the stories of children and young people tell themselves about their lives and lived experiences should take centre-stage. Each voice should be offered equal soundscape. Clearly, given an appropriate platform, children and young people can demonstrate active agency through voice and action for quite simply, we believe that the recognition of social competency and agency of those who have unconventional voices is ethically vital.

## Reflexive re-positioning

The increased emphasis on rights has challenged researchers to recognise the importance of the inclusion of children's own views. Therefore, in order to gain a perceptual grasp of the complex influences of social contexts on the young people's lives, understandings of childhoods must be anchored in their own accounts. Without including stories told by the children themselves, we believe that narratives of passivity and incompetence will remain unchallenged. The following extract from Allison's field notes supports this shift in recognition as it illustrates the ways in which a young participant resisted the ascribed position of incompetent by creatively drawing on specific resources available to her. A research conversation with this young person helped Allison understand some specific aspects of her expertise. As she competently demonstrated how she signed, the ways she used her writing board, her high-tech communication aid and her voice, she clearly illustrated that not only did she have a vast range of communication techniques but also that she was able to adopt them accordingly: depending on how she felt and who she was communicating with. She clearly enumerated her likes, her needs and her beliefs and she could express describe herself through actions. Her confidence was impressive and Allison commented on her expertise, to which she replied modestly: 'I'm not an expert, but my friend is. I'm only a little expert in comparison!' Her sense of self as a knowledgeable agent is illustrative of Giddens' (1991a) concept of reflexivity. She demonstrated her ability to read cultural life and its textured flow of social interaction in a way that her actions and explanations were constitutive of what she did and how she did it. Her concept of self as a knowledgeable agent links to Giddens' (1991a) work on self-identity and also to Goffman's (1959) suggestion that knowledgeability is tied up with thousands of other interpersonal settings and through the ways in which day-to-day life is organised. As discussed earlier, disabled children and young people are often positioned as incompetent and dependent but we believe that those with little or no voice have plenty to tell us. If appropriate and equal opportunities to speak are offered, a whole range of voices will be heard.

Mead's (1974) broad interpretation of the social nature of the construction of self whereby each of us fashions our sense of self through engagement with others can be usefully applied here. The narratives within this chapter clearly demonstrate that children routinely (re)construct themselves through their everyday experiences. Indeed, as Elliott (2008) argues, to possess 'self' implies an ability to take one's own actions, emotions and beliefs as a unified structure as well as acknowledging the perspective of the self from significant others. While some of the previous discussions have signified systems of identification as oppressive and limiting, the latter discussions demonstrate the ways in which situated agents reflexively engage with their contexts to build their sense of self. This demonstrates that each of the young participants carry around stores of unique knowledge of both external and internal structures in their heads. Neither is prioritised but both are used reflexively within specific social contexts to shape their position practice. Allison's recollection of a conversation she had with one young participant, Lizzie might be useful to further our understanding of this.

While negotiating schedules for carrying out semi-structured interviews with some of the young participants, a member of staff warned Allison that one particular girl was uncommunicative and likely to 'kick off at the slightest upset'. Indeed, during the familiarisation visits, Lizzie chose neither to look at Allison nor communicate directly with her. However, having established she was happy to take part in the interview, the teacher indicated that we might find it easier to concentrate if they went out of the noisy classroom and into the corridor. Allison was reminded of Lizzie's response signals before they left the classroom: a mixture of facial expressions, body movement and pre-recorded responses on the AACS would be used to participate in the conversations. Once they were settled, Allison started off the conversation and confirmed that Lizzie was still willing to participate in the research:

Allison: 'Hi Lizzie, are you happy to talk to me today?'
Lizzie: [moves her head to the left which activates the head switch, 'yes']
Allison: 'Thank you. Is it ok if I use my recorder?'
Lizzie: [moves her head to the left]
Allison: 'If at any time you want to stop talking to me, you can tell me to stop, or signal me to stop – is that ok?'
Lizzie: [pushes her head impatiently towards the head switch] 'Questions.' [pre-recorded message]
Allison: 'OK, time for questions!'
Lizzie: 'Where are we going?' [pre-recorded message]
Allison: 'Well, if its ok with you, we are staying here in the corridor next to your classroom, is that ok with you?'
Lizzie: [inclines her head to the left; this means 'yes']
Allison: 'Yeah, we're just parked up here to stay in this quiet corridor so we can talk, ok?'
Lizzie: [inclines her head to the left]
Allison: 'Great... Lizzie, what do you...'
Lizzie: [interrupts me with a pre-recorded message] 'Where do you live?'
Allison: 'Where do I live? I live in...'
Lizzie: [pause] 'By the sea?' [pre-recorded message]
Allison: 'Yeah, by the sea. Have you ever been there?'
Lizzie: [inclines her head to the left]
Allison: 'What did you think of it?'
Lizzie: [activates the head switch and scans the screen for her choice of reply... I wait... 'dump']

Allison: 'Oh! Right!' [I laugh] 'Well, its ok when the sun shines but I agree it is a bit miserable when it's raining! I wait a while and then start the question again. Lizzie, what do you...'
Lizzie: [she interrupts again with a pre-recorded response] 'How old are you?'
Allison: [I chuckle and answer] "45 but don't you dare tell anyone!'
Lizzie: [smiles and wriggles around a bit in her wheelchair]
Allison: 'All these questions, Lizzie – I'm supposed to be the one asking you questions!!!!'
Lizzie: [smiles and turns her head towards me]

The above extract demonstrates how the capability for autonomous thought and reflexivity not only permits some sort of 'regrooving' of the self in the broader context, but also emphasises the importance of examining positional identities from a variety of perspectives. Indeed, had this discussion relied merely on the interpretation of the observations undertaken and on the adult-led conversations in relation to this particular young person, Allison might not have interviewed her and a great deal of rich description in relation to her identity and agency would have remained undiscovered. As a result, conventional voices, or those that were easier to listen to would have been privileged and unconventional voices, or those that are require different listening skills, would have been marginalised or silenced.

Allison concluded that on the whole, while the observations and the interviews with adults were worthwhile (see in addition discussions of gatekeepers in Chapter 2) for gaining background information about the disabled children and young people and allowed her to build up a picture of the ways in which they used high-tech communication aids on a daily basis, without the narratives of the young participants themselves, opportunities to gain a more holistic understanding of their lives and an insight into their individual characters would have been lost.

Routes to hearing some voices, as Allison's research indicates, can be challenging to navigate and require a willingness and capacity to find paths through power relations embedded in the social contexts through which voices emerge. The power to speak, or remain silent are part of the socially embedded processes by which some voices are listened to, afforded greater legitimacy than others or indeed have the privilege to be heard at all. This does not just apply to the voices of participants but also, crucially, to the voices of researchers, notably those seeking to explore the construction of knowledge in contested arenas as we explore below.

## Hegemony of voice: The process of privileging

In arenas where Jessica has presented her work on sexualisation and childhood, where what is advocated is a less sensationalist and 'risk-based' approach to children's worlds, she has been approached afterwards by fellow academics who have dubbed her brave for embarking on discussions of such controversial topics. In addition, Jessica's workshops for practitioners on considering the positive elements of young people's sexual lives were highlighted by attendees as the only offering they had yet to experience as part of their professional development which did not focus on unplanned pregnancies, STIs and sexual exploitation and wasn't that a brave approach to take. As Goode's experiences have indicated (Channel 4 Press 2014), advocating alternative ways of thinking that depart from the dominant conversation in any given arena also have potentially very difficult consequences (see Chapter 1). What can be seen from Goode's experiences researching with self-defined 'minor attracted adults' (2010) is what we have dubbed a hegemony of voice. Her attempt, like that of Plummer (Gilligan 2014), to critically evaluate public perceptions of paedophiles as other than a dangerous, criminal perversion and as a part of the wider human condition, generated significant public outrage with an assumption that this somehow advocated sexual attraction to children. This attempt to speak in ways that extended the debate beyond this single hegemonic position led in Goode's case to disastrous consequences for her academic career. What this highlights is the potential ramifications for the construction of knowledge of the questioning of this canonical narrative (Bruner 2004).

Sarah found that her voice was limited in various ways depending on the context. In her data collection, remaining silent in the interviews was, on occasion, difficult as respondents sought to draw her in to conversation about her own adoption experiences. A further dynamic that Sarah experienced was that discussing her research in other arenas was not always easy. In a review of adoption and race literature, Kirton (1996, see also Högbacka 2013) remarks about the lack of disclosure on the part of researchers to identify themselves as intercountry or transracial adopters.

Rastas (2005 in Yngvesson 2010:33) claims that it remains problematic for intercountry adoptive parents to discuss their motivations to adopt as such decisions are invariably perceived as racist. Gaber and Aldridge (1994:1) provide further explanations of their silence by claiming that any proponent of transracial adoption runs the risk of being castigated as racist, which effectively makes 'further argument unnecessary'. It is therefore unsurprising that many adopters remain cautious about revealing or discussing their families.

Sarah's personal position in her study emerged as being an important epistemological aspect, and therefore it was necessary and important to identify her proximity to the research subject. However, she recognised why others may feel reticent to do so and experienced trepidation in identifying this personal involvement. As part of her research Sarah attended a number of conferences, which discussed the issues surrounding transracial and intercountry adoption. Despite numerous opportunities, she never felt able to disclose her status as an intercountry adopter at these conferences or contribute in ways that would disclose this status. In part, this was due to the negative connotations attached to intercountry adoption and intercountry adopters, but she also felt that any contribution she might make would then only be perceived through her own mothering choices. Her voice in this arena was silenced, to some extent a self-induced silence, in part by the dominance of ideas which argue that parents of transracially adopted child are insufficiently equipped to assist children manage their experiences of racism in an 'inherently racist' world (Barn 2000; Triseliotis et al., 1997:164). As intercountry adopters of a transracially adopted children, parents like Sarah are openly spoken about but far less often heard in this regard. In consequence the activities that these families do engage in to support their children in this regard remain for the most part unheard which is to the deficit of a wider debate about how to support transracially and intercountry adopted children.

Approaches to intercountry adoption, and indeed many other topics, are shaped by dominant discourses whereby particular knowledge and positions are privileged, and these positions become canonical narratives (Bruner 2004). These narratives shape the way a topic can be discussed, written and thought about, determining what is acceptable to say, it thus becomes the moral order. Part of the silencing of voices in some debates can also be linked to the category entitlement or lack of entitlement of some to be seen to legitimately contribute to the debate.

Phoenix (2008:66) uses category entitlement to analyse the ways in which one of her respondents 'a white mother of adult children of mixed parentage' establishes her entitlement to speak of her knowledge and experiences of racism to Phoenix as a 'black woman, in a study of social identities' (ibid.). Phoenix describes how this respondent uses stories to position herself as knowledgeable of racism and presents herself as being against racism. This perspective is further emphasised by the stories of how she parents her children. The stories the respondent tells construct her as learning to stand up against racism even in the face of injury or harm. Phoenix describes these stories as moral and part of how the respondent constructs herself as a 'hero', holding a world view of 'racism as illegitimate' (2008:69). The respondent uses her stories to position herself as holding legitimate authority to discuss racism.

Perhaps it is the absence of the opportunity to establish such an entitlement to speak that mutes voices, either the absence of related experience or the opportunity to share these experiences because of how the canonical narratives are constructed. Hydén (2008:125) argues that 'without having experienced the cognitive process of 'having been through' an experience so that 'you know about it', it is difficult to discuss the experience.'

In the case of research in the field of disability studies some scholars argue that disability discourses are still dominated by people who are not disabled (Kitchin 2000). Oliver (1992) finds this issue significantly problematic and concurs with Hydén in arguing that this traditional 'expert' model of research alienates, disempowers and disenfranchises disabled research participants. The interpretation of the knowledge and experience of disabled individuals by 'non-disabled' researchers is 'compounding the oppression of disabled respondents' (Kitchin 2000:26). A comparison could be made here to the voices of children in the research process which come to subsequently be collected, interpreted and thus dominated by adult researchers (Coad and Evans 2008). Increasing interest in child-centred methodologies has led to the advocating of children as peer researchers involved in all aspects of the research process from design to data analysis. Such approaches attempt to address the imbalance of power relations in research with children (Christensen and James 2000) by attempting to give children greater degrees of control over the research process (Thomas and O'Kane 1998). However, notions of empowerment and of power itself are far more slippery (Foucault 1995) and nebulous than these approaches suggest. Power is negotiated and co-constructed in social interactions rather than existing as a static and structural phenomenon. Therefore, while we do not hold to Hydén's and Oliver's arguments that such experiential knowledge is necessary before empathy and understanding can occur, we do concur with Phoenix (2008) in that our own particular attributes and experiences can award category entitlement which legitimises not only the authority to speak, but also the power to co-construct the narratives told.

What can be seen from the examples above is an active demonstration of the hegemony of voice whereby particular positions and arguments privilege or marginalise both what is being said and by who. Just as researchers are often attributed the position of 'expert' on a topic (Danieli and Woodhams 2005) by the very virtue of their status as questioner the positions they simultaneously occupy as mother, woman, professional practitioner to name but a few can render them vulnerable. This vulnerability results in the potential of having our voices labelled as flawed because we reveal ourselves to not just (or at all) being experts but rather subjects who are part of the co-construction of knowledge and either don't display the objectivity still often desired within social science research, having views which are shaped by more than just the label of researcher or by deeming to speak in ways that are at odds with dominant knowledge in our fields.

## Conclusion

The discussions within this chapter have clearly demonstrated the ways in which young participants' voices are embedded in external structures of power, difference, entitlement and social affiliation. While acknowledging the importance in recognising the rights of children and empowering them to express their views in matters that concern them, we have argued that is it equally important that we value and include *all* voices, not just those that are easy to hear and interpret. The scenarios have illustrated that listening is a skill necessary for researchers to acquire in order that they become part of the in situ conversations, for we found that the ones that we were privileged to be included in revealed that the children and young people have much to say.

The rush to hear voices has masked the scrutiny needed to listen and we therefore argue for a more critical recognition of the ways in which unconventional voices are shaped and constructed by historical and cultural perceptions of disability. However, as this chapter draws to a close, we are reminded of Jackson's (2003) cautionary advice. While clearly advocating working hard against the limits of voice in order to hear those that have been silenced, she warns us to resist the temptation to echo one's own voice in silent data or filling those silences with yet another voice of our own desires.

# Conclusion

Specific stories have been presented within this book whose aim is to capture a glimpse of a world beyond the normative constructions of what ethical research with children looks like. We have stepped beyond the boundaries of topic, interrogated discursive and structural motifs of childhood itself, reflected upon our own roles and identities in the research process and questioned the construction and application of ethics and ethical principles. The stories we tell reflect upon the juxtapositions inherent between the ethical principles that currently guide research with children and the practical realities of such endeavours. Having to confront paradoxes of position, power, voice and topic, to name but a few, means that we inevitably challenge orthodox methodological discussions about ethics. It is in the telling of such stories that we seek to move ethical understandings further.

The involvement of children in research has become a canonical narrative which carries certain key concepts such as empowerment, agency, rights and participation, all of which build an ethical mirage where these concepts, once articulated, go underexplored and unreflected. The paradigm shift which brought 'child-centred' research into common practice challenged previous assumptions about childhood and children's capacities and attributes, allowing for their greater involvement and inclusion. However, much research with children neglects to interrogate how these concepts or 'cherished conceits' (Segal 1999) have been defined, how they are practised by individual children in their research experiences and how they are used by researchers. These ideas have thus become part of the established habitus – the moral order which informs current research practice to be followed and unquestioned. We are certainly not advocating a return to previous practices with children in research nor that concepts such as agency and participation not be integral to our methodologies. But we challenge the lack of debate about how these concepts are defined and performed by children in research. One example of this can be found in Chapter 4 where we discuss how children exert relational agency within the relationships and in the social contexts where they are situated. Wim, for example, a participant in Sarah's research, consistently used her relational agency to situate Sarah in the position of authority in the interview and indeed laughed when Sarah claimed that Wim was in charge. Sarah was variously positioned as researcher, teacher or mother in her interviews with the young girls in her research. These relational positions were co-constructed with her participants (Mishler 1986) and demonstrate the capacity of these girls to negotiate with adults to assert themselves to their advantage and comfort without challenging the normative power relations between adults or child that an autonomy of selfhood (Walkerdine 1989) would induce.

The neglect of reflecting on the ways that dominant attributes of childhood are articulated, or resisted, inhibits our understandings of the ways in which children exert power in their relationships and the ways in which they participate in social interactions which might challenge the conventional definitions of the very concepts that inform our practice towards children. Such knowledge can be lost to us by ignoring, in this case, the social context of research itself, and what remains are disembodied children's voices, abstracted from the social context in which they emerged and were performed. 'Voice' has thus become the catchword used to imply all of the key concepts above but with little or no reflection on the embedded power relations, the positionalities and identities being performed in the spaces and places where these voices were heard. Such nebulous cobwebs of social interaction are all too often swept away in our desire for sanitised research narratives when their inclusion could further our understanding of how children demonstrated these skills in their social relations. How identities commonly attributed to children in research (indeed these attributes are often the only reason the children are included in our research), such as pupil, daughter, sister, adoptee, disabled, innocent, vulnerable, agentic, are complied with, adapted or resisted by children in our research endeavours are stories often left unheard. The stories told here say little about our individual research topics but instead highlight ways in which children are active in negotiating their particular social contexts. They reveal ways in which children exert a relational agency built less on our 'cherished conceits' and 'persistent illusions' (Segal 1999:110), concerning the attributes of childhood and more about children's capacity to transcend assumed attributes and deficits, and instead use refined skills of managing complex and dynamic social relationships. As such they highlight little concerning children's autonomy and independence but much on their use of interdependency and social agency. As researchers, we should include rather than evade such stories in our discussions as pivotal in furthering our understanding of not just what children say and do but how and why they say it – the social context which shapes their voices.

When assumptions regarding agency, voice and indeed childhood itself remain uninterrogated, when they are not considered as situated and embedded, the result is a homogenous treatment of all research with children. What is often advocated as a result of the paradigmatic shift towards research with children, as discussed above, is 'child-centred' approaches to research and what are made are claims that we are thus capturing the voices of the agentic child. Such shifts are important in recognising children in research as subjects, not objects; however, what we have witnessed in our experiences is that claims of 'child-centredness' are often under-examined and clear boundaries still exist regarding how, when, why and what children are allowed to speak about. Just as Danieli and Woodhams (2005) argue that the social model of disability has in some ways come to dominate conversations about disability to the exclusion of other perspectives, we argue here that child-centred research has become a catch-all phrase for what is perceived as 'good' research with few having the courage or indeed impetus to question some of the assumptions it is founded upon.

Philosophical assumptions regarding children's capabilities to contribute to the construction of knowledge may have shifted within particular domains, for example, regarding their views on education or play but still remain limited in areas constructed as taboo or out of bounds. Certain topics, as we have explored here, such as adoption and non-normative family formation, gendered and sexual identities or disabilities, are considered as sensitive to explore, particularly in relation to children. This we argue is a direct result of the key tropes that abound of childhood itself whereby adults are uncomfortable hearing the views and experiences of beings whom are constructed as intrinsically innocent (Faulkner 2011). The manifestation of this innocence is context-bound and such imagery thus varies, we may worry about and/or pity the orphaned child, the sexual child, the street child, the asylum seeking child, the disabled child but what all of these tropes have in common is the positioning of these children's experiences as outside of normative childhoods. Such classifications are placed before the category of childhood and children are consequently marginalised and othered by this categorisation. Asking children to speak within such arenas thus generates anxiety despite the fact that for these children what they are being asked to share is their own experiences, elements of their own lives, which often they do not view as taboo at all. We argue that more attention needs to be paid to the voices of children within domains where they remain ignored due to some perceived assault on adult expectations of sensitivity or vulnerability. We do not advocate talking to children (or indeed adults) in ways that may cause them harm or distress but what we do argue is that the entire notion of 'sensitive' topics requires a much greater degree of interrogation. Such definitions have profound implications for research participants and researchers alike.

It is through articulations of power that particular positions are privileged or indeed marginalised. If even the topic that we are allowed to ask about and that children are allowed to respond to, is governed by the social order of both research with children and childhood itself then all aspects of the research process must be conceptualised as influenced by socially embedded power relations. Here Foucauldian notions of power relations (Foucault 1972, 1995) are useful in understanding its fluidity in research encounters. Assumptions in research with children are often made regarding dichotomies of power whereby adults are powerful and children are powerless, yet what our stories here reveal is the complex ways in which power is established, negotiated and articulated by all parties through ideas such as category entitlement and interdependency. Children's social agency in these encounters is not easily contained within a category of 'powerless' or 'dependent' and as such we should not naively assume that our approaches, values and methods, however ideal in their intention, necessarily work to empower children or to elevate their voices. Indeed in many situations we as adults occupy a position of 'powerlessness', as explored for example in Chapter 2, whereby the need to maintain guest relations in schools and homes places researchers in difficult and often subordinate positions. Despite assumptions, we do not, cannot and are not always occupying the position of 'expert' and our attempts to hand this position to children themselves are also far from straightforward and not necessarily always ethical. Problematising assumptions relating to the positions that individuals occupy and strategies they may make use of in research encounters is crucial to understanding research relationships and the construction of data itself. For example, there is an assumption that the empowered child is the child who speaks, but as our stories illustrate, children make effective use of silence as a strategy of power in social relations (Lewis 2008).

The fluidity of power in research relations is however not actively acknowledged in the governance of research itself. The tendency of RECs is to adopt risk-averse approaches to research with children and young people in the name of protection. Such positioning is in direct contradiction to the elevation of children's voices articulated in rights documentation and academic discourse whereby their agentic participation is considered paramount. Researchers' thus seeking this agentic child, the child as being, the child as expert, face a difficult challenge where they must in ethics documentation emphasise the vulnerable child in need of protection but methodologically seek to hear the voices of agentic children. RECs which emphasise assent over consent or view particular topics as problematic, even illegitimate, can thus come to be seen as barriers which researchers must overcome rather than resources which can support the conduct of ethical research. A tendency towards procedural ethics promotes a desire to present only sanitised narratives of research whereby the messiness, relational and situational elements of such encounters and relationships is not accounted for (Guillemin and Gillam 2004).

In this book we have used the concepts of category membership and entitlement to demonstrate the ways in which respondents in our research established their authority to speak about topics. The capacity to ask questions, to answer and to understand the social interactions on a given topic are all developed through conversations where we each legitimise our stories through the categories we claim or are attributed to us. As Lawler (2014) argues, stories are used to produce our identities. Category memberships are created through discourse and allow us to anticipate the reception our stories will receive and shape how we tell them to the audience present. Stories told to Sarah by adoptive mothers were informed by the knowledge that she was also an adoptive mother. Her membership of this category allowed respondents to understand her interest as well as assist them in determining whether or not to take part. As seen in Chapter 5, the girls telling their adoptive stories also used category membership, both accepting and resisting attributed identity traits, as illustrated by Mel's (and others) claim 'I am more than just adopted'. In addition in Chapters 3 and 6, Allison told stories incited by her research which examined the physical and attitudinal restrictions imposed on particular children's voices by virtue of assumed attributes and deficits. Here we also saw young people's active resistance of such categorisations.

Often, in order to establish an entitlement to speak as a member of a particular category self-disclosure is used. Indeed, self-disclosure is actually productive in Sarah's research relations. Through openly discussing, when asked, her status as an intercountry adoptive mother she set out to reassure young respondents through such discourse and at least one girl took part as a result of such self-disclosure. As Sarah identified, the dilemma in this instance about whether self-disclosure made it easier for this respondent to say yes or harder for her to say no, remains unresolved. As indicated in Chapters 2 and 6, not disclosing stories about her own adoption and mothering experiences proved to be an issue in her interviews. This of course is in part related to the method and methodology selected. Semi-structured interviews where stories are co-constructed hold elements of culturally expected reciprocity particularly in relation to women (Holmes 1997), described by Oakley (1981) as being, when our questions are asked back. The balance between a researcher and member of a particular group can be challenging to maintain when intimate stories are being shared.

Such a balance is further complicated by the spaces where the research takes place. As Jordan (2006) has argued, the relationships between researcher and respondent are more ambiguous in the intimate spaces such as the home. The social conventions surrounding relations in the home ensure that researchers arrive as guests and are often perceived as being first and foremost a guest in the home (Yee and Andrew 2006). Moving beyond this category can be challenging for the researcher and the interviewee (Bird 2003). Such intricate relations are common to each social context but performed in unique ways which are not possible to anticipate prior to the interview. Mayall (2000b) describes these relations as a triangle of conventions. As we discuss in Chapter 2, such conventions shape the data in multiple ways. Sarah illustrates how negative characteristics commonly attributed to intercountry adopters such as neo-liberal consumer accessing a market (Dickens 2012), are reconstructed by an interviewee into the very qualities required to progress through an intrusive and overly bureaucratic system. Such careful identity construction is inextricably linked to the location in which this interview took place (Sarah's home) and the category memberships of those involved; a social worker and an intercountry adopter. To ignore the social context in which these voices are heard and the category memberships which inform the ways these stories are told is not only to sanitise them, but undermine the very complexity of social research. As we argue in Chapter 4, unless we include the 'backdrop of [our] interpretations' (Elliott 2005:183), more commonly in research with children, then the social embeddedness of children's agency, and their capacity to exert it, is lost.

As Sin (2005) argues, issues such as informed consent can seldom, if ever, be disconnected from the social context in which permission is sought. This is further complicated by the social positioning of children within the social context and subsequently in research. This positioning is exemplified by the issue of informed consent. In considering the positioning of children as unable to provide full informed consent, where some use the alternative of 'assent' (as discussed in Chapter 1), we were presented with a motif of children as irrational beings without the desired capacity to participate fully in social life. We argue that this is an unacceptable classification of children as incapable subjects which reinforces the perpetual 'othering' of children within the research process (Lahman 2008) and such practices contribute to the more general powerlessness of children under an adult gaze. The risk here is that as a result of dominant developmental frameworks which emphasise not an existing but a growing capacity to engage in decision-making children become objectified as passive social objects (Clark 2014). This includes the ability to process information about and consent to participating in social research. However, we argue that positions such as these fail to recognise the extent to which even very young children engage in decision making, whereby morality is part of the everyday life of all human beings (see Mayall 2002).

Where informed consent is not required or deemed appropriate it is still common to see the phrase assent used to define the confirmation of children's participation in research. Assent is defined as the child's permission or affirmation of agreement to participate in research (Broome and Richards 1998) and is regarded by some researchers as a substitute for consent so that children do not consent in their own right but assent to their parent's consent (Powell and Smith 2010). We have questioned whether the upholding of dignity, highlighted in many ethical guidelines (BERA 2011; BSA 2002; ESRC 2012) and in key human rights instruments (Bell 2008), can be maintained while positioning children's agreement as lesser than that of adults within the research process; a position which 'fails to accord them the same rights as adults in terms of what their consent means' (Skelton 2008:23).

What we risk when we construct children and young people's 'consent' as somehow lesser than adults is the privileging of particular voices over others. We maintain the status quo of children as objects of research, which was supposed to be overturned by the introduction and now dominance of participatory methods. This is particularly the case for groups of children categorised as particularly vulnerable by virtue of ascribed characteristics (such as the disabled child, the adopted child, the sexualised child). As Allison's research demonstrates the children and young people who participated in her study where the last to be consulted in a long and intricate 'chain of consent'. This chain was directly related to the networks of power belonging to particular adults surrounding the children, from head teacher to class teachers to parents and finally, to the children. Jessica's experiences being guided away from online research with children and young people (discussed in Chapter 2) mirror this concern regarding the desire to but complexities of gaining authentic informed consent from children and adults in particular spaces. The result of such classifications is that particular stories are more readily accessed and thus more readily heard.

As Frank (2010) argues, stories accompany us through life, from birth to death, they entertain, educate and can inform us about right and wrong and show us who we are. The stories we share within this book illustrate how we applied, questioned and critiqued ethical procedures and principles and made decisions in the moment according to the situation and the social contexts we found ourselves in. Such stories of course are not new in qualitative research; they are even emerging in quantitative research (Elliot 2005). But we suggest that they are as yet, underexploited in research with children. The imperative to be ethical and be seen to be ethical when involving children, may act as a deterrent for researchers in telling stories which reveal the doing of ethics to be more ambiguous and socially situated than textbooks imply. Or that agency and empowerment are less straightforward to evoke in our endeavours than the definitions and aspirations suggest. Or that capturing the 'voice' of the child is enough when what subsequently evades us are the children themselves.

We celebrate those who came before us and successfully challenged the assumed passivity and incapacities of children so explicit in previous approaches to research *on* children. But we suggest that the contemporary social order through which participatory research with children is organised and delivered now needs greater critical reflection. Doing ethics, being ethical, does not begin or end with a signed form and permission from an ethics committee, this is merely the beginning. Research is messy, it is fractured and it is imperfect. These stories are also messy, they represent our stories of the ethical decisions we made and as such they are not presented as 'right' or 'wrong'. Rather as multiple, contingent, hidden and context-bound. Although we, as authors, have in common similar values about research with children and a shared vision of what it should look like and we have articulated them here, we recognise that when we seek to shine a light on these dark spaces we will thus create shadows elsewhere. As such by sharing these narratives, our hope is not to provide a guidebook for the conducting of research with children but that other researchers are encouraged to tell their own stories, to make their own unique decisions in their own moments and to move beyond a simplistic dichotomy of 'good' or 'bad' research and 'right' or 'wrong' ethics.

# References

Aapola, S., Gonick, A. and Harris, A. (2004) *Young Femininity: Girlhood, Power and Social Change*, Basingstoke: Palgrave Macmillan

Aarsan, P. A. and Aronsson, K. (2009) 'Gaming and Territorial Negotiations in Family Life' *Childhood*, vol.16(4), 497–517

Abebe, T. and Bessell, S. (2014) 'Advancing Ethical Research with Children: Critical Reflections on Ethical Guidelines' *Children's Geographies*, vol.12(1), 126–133

Abell, J., Locke, A., Condor, S., Gibson, S. and Stevenson, C. (2006) 'Trying Similarity, Doing Difference: The Role of Interviewer Self-Disclosure in Interview Talk with Young People' *Qualitative Research*, vol.6(2), 221–244

Agar, M. H (1980) *The Professional Stranger*, New York: Academic Press

Alderson, P. (1995) *Listening to Children*, London: Barnardos

Alderson, P. and Goodey C. (1996) 'Research with Disabled Children: How Useful Is Child-Centred Ethics?' *Children and Society*, vol.10(2), 106–116

Alderson, P. and Montgomery, J. (1996) *Healthcare Choices: Making Decisions with Children*, London: Institute for Public Policy Research

Alderson, P. and Morrow, V. (2006) 'Multi-Disciplinary Research Ethics Review: Is It Feasible?' *International Journal of Social Research Methodology: Theory and Practice*, vol.9, 405–417

Allan, G. and Crow, G. (2001) *Families, Households and Society*, Basingstoke: Palgrave Macmillan

Alleyne, B. (2015) *Narrative Networks: Storied Approaches in a Digital Age*, London: Sage

Alvesson, M., Ashcraft, K. L. and Thomas, R. (2008) 'Identity Matters: Reflections on the Construction of Identity Scholarship in Organization Studies' *Organization*, vol.15, 5–28

Alvesson, M. and Sköldberg, K. (2009) *Reflexive Methodology* (2nd ed.), Los Angeles: Sage

Andrews, M. (2008) Never the Last Word: Revisiting Data, in Andrews, M., Squire, C. and Tamboukou, M. (eds.) *Doing Narrative Research*, London: Sage, 86–102

Andrews, M., Squires, C. and Tamboukou, M. (eds.) (2008) *Doing Narrative Research*, London: Sage

Anzil, V. (2013) 'Adopting "Imaginaries": International Adoption in the Spanish Press' *Adoption & Fostering*, vol.37(1), 71–82

Archard, D. (2004) *Children: Rights and Childhood* (2nd ed.), London: Routledge

Atkinson, P. and Coffey, A. (2003) Revisiting the Relationship Between Participant Observation and Interviewing, in Gubrium, J. F. and Holstein, J. A. (eds.) *Postmodern Interviewing*, London: Sage, 109–122

Aull Davies, C. (2008) *Reflexive Ethnography: A Guide to Researching Selves and Others* (2nd ed.), London: Routledge

Badham, B. (2004) 'Participation – for a Change: Disabled Young People Lead the Way' *Children and Society*, vol.18, 143–154

Baker, C. D. (2003) Ethnomethodological Analyses of Interviews, in Holstein, J. A. and Gubrium, J. F. (eds.) *Inside Interviewing New Lenses, New Concerns*, London: Sage, 395–412

Barker, J. and Smith, F. (2001) 'Power, Positionality and Practicality: Carrying Out Fieldwork with Children' *Ethics, Place and Environment: A Journal of Philosophy and Geography*, vol.4(2), 142–147

Barker, J. and Weller, S. (2003) 'Never Work with Children? The Geography of Methodological Issues in Research with Children' *Qualitative Research*, vol.3(2), 207–227

Barn, R. (2000) Race, Ethnicity and Transracial Adoption, in Katz, I. and Treacher, A. (eds.) *The Dynamics of Adoption*, London: Jessica Kingsley Publishers, 101–125

Barn, R. and Kirton, D. (2012) Transracial Adoption in Britain Politics, Ideology and Reality, in Phoenix, A. and Simmonds, J. (eds.) *Multiculturalism, Identity and Family Placement, Adoption & Fostering*, vol.36(3–4), 25–37

Barthes, R. (1977) *Music, Image, Text, Trans. Stephen Heath*, London: Fontana Press

Bartholet, E. (1999) *Family Bonds: Adoption, Infertility and the New World of Child Production*, Boston: Beacon Press

Basset, E. and O'Riordan, K. (2002) 'Ethics of Internet Research: Contesting the Human Subjects Research Model' *Ethics and Information Technology*, vol.4(3), 233–247

Beck, U. (1992) *Risk Society: Towards a New Modernity*, London: Sage

Benatar, S. (2002) 'Reflections and Recommendations on Research Ethics in Developing Countries' *Social Science and Medicine*, vol.54, 1131–1141

BERA (British Educational Research Association) (2011) Ethical Guidelines for Educational Research, Available at: www.bera.ac.uk/publications/ethical -guidelines [Accessed: 29th January 2015]

Bell, N. (2008) 'Ethics in Child Research: Rights, Reason and Responsibilities' *Children's Geographies*, vol.6(1), 7–20

Bell, C. and Newby, H. (1977) *Doing Sociological Research*, London: Allen and Unwin

Bell, C. C. and Roberts, H. (eds.) (1984) *Social Researching: Politics, Problems, Practice*, London: Routledge & Kegan Paul

Bhavnani, K. (1991) *Talking Politics: A Psychological Framing of Views from Youth in Britain*, Cambridge: Cambridge University Press

Bird, S. E. (2003) *The Audience in Everyday Life: Living in a Media World*, New York: Routledge

Bluebond-Langner, M. (1978) *The Private World of Dying Children*, Princeton, NJ: Princeton University Press

Boden, R. and Epstein, D. (2006) 'Managing the Research Imagination? Globalisation and Research in Higher Education' *Globalisation, Societies and Education*, vol.4(2), 223–236

Boden, R., Epstein, D. and Latimer, J. (2009) 'Accounting for Ethos or Programmes for Conduct? The Brave New World of Research Ethics Committees' *The Sociological Review*, vol.57(4), 728–749

Boggis, A. (2011) 'Deafening Silences: Researching with Inarticulate Children' *Disability Studies Quarterly*, vol.31(4)

Borland, M. A. Laybourn, M. Hill and Brown, J. (1998) *Middle Childhood: The Perspectives of Children and Parents*, London: Jessica Kingsley

Bourdieu, P. (1977) *Outline of a Theory of Practice*, Cambridge: Cambridge University Press

Bourdieu, P. (1986a) *Distinction*, London: Routledge

Bourdieu, P. (1986b) 'From Rules to Strategies' *Cultural Anthropology*, vol.1, 110–120

Brooks, R., te Riele, K. and Maguire, M. (2014) *Ethics and Education Research*, London: Sage

Broome, M. and Richards, D. (1998) 'Involving Children in Research' *Journal of Child and Family Nursing*, vol.1(1), 3–7

BSA (British Sociological Association) (2002) Statement of Ethical Practice, Available at: www.britsoc.co.uk/about/equality/statement-of-ethical-practice.aspx [Accessed: 29th January 2015]

Bruckman, A. (2002) 'Studying the Amateur Artist: A Perspective on Disguising Data Collected in Human Subjects Research on the Internet' *Ethics and Information Technology*, vol.4(3), 217–231

Bruner, J. (2004) 'Life as Narrative' *Social Research*, vol.71(3), 691–710

Bryson, M. and de Castell, S. (1994) 'Telling Tales Out of School: Modernist, Critical, and Postmodern True Stories about Educational Computing' *Journal of Educational Computing Research*, vol.10, 199–221

Butler, I. and Williamson, H. (1994) *Children Speak: Children, Trauma and Social Work*, London: Longman

Cameron, L. and Murphey, J. (2006) 'Obtaining Consent to Participate in Research: The Issues Involved in Including People with a Range of Learning and Communication Disabilities' *British Journal of Learning Disabilities*, vol.35, 113–120

Carlson, C. (2004) What Is Performance?, in Bial, H. (ed) *The Performance Studies Reader* (2nd ed.), London: Routledge, 70–75

Cavet, J. and Sloper, P. (2004) 'Participation of Disabled Children in Individual Decisions About Their Lives and in Public Decisions about Service Development' *Children and Society*, vol.18, 278–290

Cerulo, K. (1997) 'Identity Construction: New Issues, New Directions' *Annual Review of Sociology*, vol.23, 385–409

Channel 4 Press (2014) 'The Paedophile Next Door' Available at: http://www.channel4.com/info/press/programme-information/the-paedophile-next-door [Accessed: 21st January 2015]

Children Act 1989, London: HMSO

Children (Scotland) Act, 1995

Children (Northern Ireland) Order, 1995

Childwise (2013) *Report: Trends in Media Use, Research Highlights for Children's Online Safety 50*, Available at: http://www.saferinternet.org.uk/content /childnet/safterinternetcentre/downloads/Research_Highlights/UKCCIS _RH50_Childwise_Trends_Report.pdf [Accessed: 21st January 2015]

Christensen, P. (1999) Towards an Anthropology of Childhood Sickness: an Ethnographic Study of Danish School Children. PhD Thesis, University of Hull

Christensen, P. and James, A. (2000) *Research with Children: Perspectives and Practices*, London: Falmer Press

Christensen, P. and James, A. (2001) What Are Schools for? The Temporal Experience of Children's Learning in Northern England, in Alanen, L. and Mayall, B. (eds.) *Conceptualising Child-Adult Relations*, London: Routledge, 70–85

Christensen, P. and Prout, A. (2002) 'Working with Ethical Symmetry in Social Research with Children' *Childhood*, vol.9(4), 477–497

Clark, J. (2013a) 'Passive, Heterosexual and Female: Constructing Appropriate Childhoods in the Sexualisation of Childhood Debate' *Sociological Research Online*, vol.18(2), Available at Accessed: http://www.socresonline.org.uk/18/ 2/13.html

Clark, J. (2013b) Children's Geographies, in Taylor, J., Bond, E. and Woods, M. (eds.) *Early Childhood Studies: A Multidisciplinary and Holistic Introduction*, London: Hodder, 272–292

Clark, J. (2014) Sexualisation and the Discursive Figure of the Child, in Warehime, M. N. (ed) *Soul of Society: A Focus on the Lives of Children and Youth, Sociological Studies of Children and Youth*, vol.18, Bingley: Emerald Publishing, 173–197

Coad, J. and Evans, R. (2008) 'Reflections on Practical Approaches to Involving Children and Young People in the Data Analysis Process' *Children and Society*, vol.22(1), 41–52

Cockburn, T. (1998) 'Children and Citizenship in Britain: A Case for a Socially Interdependent Model of Citizenship' *Childhood*, vol.5(1), 99–117

Cockburn, T. (2005) 'Children and the Feminist Ethic of Care' *Childhood*, vol.12(1), 71–89

Code, L. (1991) *What Can She Know? Feminist Theory and the Construction of Knowledge*, New York: Cornell University Press

Coffey, A. (1999) *Ethnographic Self*, London: Sage

Collier Quy, R. (2006) Performing Childhood, in Trenka, J., Oparah J. C. and Shin S. Y. (eds.) *Outsiders Within*, Cambridge: South End Press, 213–217

Collins, R. (2004) *Interaction Ritual Chains*, Princeton, NJ: Princeton University Press

Connolly, P. (2000) Race, Gender and Critical Reflexivity in Research with Young Children, in Christensen, P. and James, A. (eds.) *Research with Children Perspectives and Practices*, London: Routledge, 173–188

Corsaro, W. A. (1997) *The Sociology of Childhood*, Thousand Oaks, CA: Pine Forges Press

Crapanzano, V. (1986) Hermes Dilemma: The Masking of Subversion in Ethnographic Description, in Marcus, G. and Clifford, J. (eds.) *Writing Culture*, Berkeley: University of California Press, 51–76

Crompton, R. (2001) 'Gender Comparative Research and Biographical Matching' *European Societies*, vol.3(2), 167–190

Conquergood, D. (1991) 'Rethinking Ethnography: Towards a Critical Cultural Politics' *Communications Monographs*, vol.58, 179–194

Conquergood, D. (2002) 'Performance Studies: Interventions and Radical Research' *The Drama Review*, vol.46(2), 145–156

Daniel, P. and Gustafsson, U. (2010) 'School Lunches: Children's Services or Children's Spaces?' *Children's Geographies*, vol.8(3), 265–274

Danieli, A. and Woodhams, C. (2005) 'Emancipatory Research and Disability: A Critique' *International Journal of Social Research Methodology*, vol.8(4), 281–296

David, M., Edwards, R. and Alldred, P. (2001) 'Children and School-Based Research: Informed Consent or Educated Consent?' *British Educational Research Journal*, vol.27(3), 347–365

Denscombe, M. and Aubrook, L. (1992) 'It's Just Another Piece of Schoolwork: The Ethics of Questionnaire Research on Pupils in Schools' *British Educational Research Journal*, vol.18, 113–131

Denzin, N. (2000) The Practices and Politics of Interpretation, in Denzin, N. K. and Lincoln Y. S. (eds.) *Handbook of Qualitative Research* (2nd ed.), Thousand Oaks, CA: Sage, 897–922

Denzin, N. K. (2003) *Performance Ethnography Critical Pedagogy and the Politics of Culture*, London: Sage

Department of Health (1991) *The Children Act 1989 Guidance and Regulations: Volume 6 Children with Disabilities*, London: Department of Health

DePalma, R. (2010) 'Socially Just Research for Social Justice: Negotiating Consent and Safety in a Participatory Action Research Project' *International Journal of Research and Method in Education*, vol.33(3), 215–227

DeSchauwer, E., Van Hove, G. and Loots, G. (2009) ' "I need help on Mondays, it's not my day. The other days, I'm ok". Perspectives of Disabled Children on Inclusive Education' *Children and Society*, vol.23, 99–111

Devine, F. and Heath, S. (1999) *Sociological Research Methods in Context*, Basingstoke: Palgrave Macmillan

Dickens, J. (2012) 'Social Policy Approaches and Social Work Dilemmas in Intercountry Adoption' in Gibbons, J. L. and Rotabi, K. S. (eds.) *Intercountry Adoption Policies, Practices, and Outcomes*, Farnham: Ashgate pp.29–42

Dingwall, R. (2008) 'The Ethical Case Against Ethical Regulation in Humanities and Social Science Research' *Twenty-First Century Society*, vol.3(1), 1–12

Dingwall, R. (2011) Absurd Decisions by Ethics Committees, Available at: www.socialsciencespace.com/2011/02/absurd-decisions-by-ethics-committees [Accessed: 29th January 2015]

Dockett, S., Perry, B., Kearney, E., Hampshire, A., Mason, J. and Schmied, V. (2009) 'Researching with Families: Ethical Issues and Situations' *Contemporary Issues in Early Childhood*, vol.10(4), 353–365

Dorow, S. (2006) *Transnational Adoption. A Cultural Economy of Race, Gender and Kinship*, New York: New York University Press

Douglas, M. (1979) Man, Myth and Magic, in Cavendish, R. (ed) *Taboo*, London: BPCC/Phoebus Publishing, 2767–2761

Douglas, M. (1991) *Purity and Danger*, London: Routledge

Drew, P. (1978) 'Accusations: The Occasioned Use of Members' Knowledge of "Religious Geography" in Describing Events' *Sociology*, vol.12(1), 1–22

Duchinsky, R. and Clark, J. The Sexualisation of Boys? Purity, Danger and Masculinity, unpublished paper

Dunbar, C., Rodriquez, D. and Parker, L. (2002) Race, Subjectivity and the Interview Process, in Gubrium, J. F. and Holstein, J. A. (eds.) *Handbook of Interview Research*, London: Sage, 279–298

Dworkin, G. (1988) *The Theory and Practice of Autonomy*, Cambridge: Cambridge University Press

Eder, D. and Fingerson, L. (2003) Interviewing Children and Adolescents, in Holstein, J. A. and Gubrium, J. F. (eds.) *Inside Interviewing: New Lenses, New Concerns*, London: Sage, 33–53

Edwards, C. and Imrie, R. (2003) 'Disability and Bodies as Bearers of Value' *Sociology*, vol.37(2), 239–256

Edwards, R. and Mauthner, M. (2012) Ethics and Feminist Research: Theory and Practice, in Miller, T., Birch, M., Mauthner, M. and Jessop, J. (eds.) *Ethics and Qualitative Research* (2nd ed.), London: Sage, 14–28

Elbers, E. (2004) 'Conversational Asymmetry and the Child's Perspective in Developmental and Educational Research' *International Journal of Disability, Development and Education*, vol.51(2), 201–205

Elliott, J. (2005) *Using Narrative in Social Research*, London: Sage

Elliott, A. (2008) *Concepts of the Self* (2nd ed.), London: Polity Press

Emirbayer, M. and Mische, A. (1998) 'What Is Agency?' *American Journal of Sociology*, vol.103(4), 962–1023

Emond, R. (2009) 'I Am All about the Future World: Cambodian Children's Views on Their Status as Orphans' *Children & Society*, vol.23(6), 407–417

Ennew, J. (1994) Time for Children or Time for Adults, in Qvortrup, J., Bardy, M., Sgritta, G. and Wintersberger, H. (eds.) *Childhood Matters Social Theory, Practice and Politics*, Aldershot: Avebury, 1–23

Ennew, J. (2005) Prisoners of Childhood: Orphans and Economic Dependency, in Qvortrup, J. (ed) *Studies in Modern Childhood: Society, Agency, Culture*, Basingstoke: Palgrave Macmillan, 128–146

ESRC (Economic and Social Research Council) (2012) Framework for Research Ethics, Available at: www.esrc.ac.uk/about-esrc/information/research-ethics .aspx [Accessed: 29th January 2015]

Faulkner, J. (2011) *The Importance of Being Innocent*, Cambridge: Cambridge University Press

Fawcett, B. (2000) *Feminist Perspectives on Disability*, Harlow: Pearson Education Ltd

Feinberg, J. (1980) The Child's Right to an Open Future, in Aiken, W. and La Follette, H. (eds.) *Whose Child? Children's Rights Parental Authority and State*, Totowa: Rowman and Littleford, 124–153

Finch, J. (1984) 'It's Great to Have Someone to Talk to': Ethics and Politics of Interviewing Women, in Bell, C. and Roberts, H. (eds.) *Social Researching: Politics, Problems, Practice*, London: Routledge and Kegan Paul, 70–87

Fine, M. (1994) Working with Hyphens: Reinventing Self and Other in Qualitative Research, in Denzin, N. K. and Lincoln, Y. S. (eds.) *Handbook of Qualitative Research*, Thousand Oaks: Sage, 70–82

Fisher, A. P. (2003) 'Still Not Quite as Good as Having Your Own: Toward a Sociology of Adoption' *Annual Review of Sociology*, vol.29, 255–276

Flewitt, R. (2005) 'Conducting Research with Young Children: Some Ethical Considerations' *Early Child Development and Care*, vol.175(6), 553–565

Foley, P. (2011) Democratic Spaces, in Foley, P. and Leverett, D. (eds.) *Children and Young People's Spaces*, Basingstoke: Palgrave Macmillan, 89–101

Foucault, M. (1972) *The Archaeology of Knowledge* (Sheridan Smith, A. M. Trans.), New York: Pantheon Books

Foucault, M. (1995) *Discipline and Punish: The Birth of the Prison*, New York: Vintage Books

Foucault, M. (1998) *The History of Sexuality: The Will to Knowledge*, London: Penguin

Frank, A. (2010) *Letting Stories Breathe: A Socio-Narratology*, London: University of Chicago Press

Frankel, S. (2012) *Children, Morality and Society*, Basingstoke: Palgrave Macmillan

Franklin, A. and Sloper, P. (2009) 'Supporting the Participation of Disabled Children and Young People in Decision-Making' *Children and Society*, vol.23, 3–15

Fraser, S., Lewis, V., Ding, S., Kellett, M. and Robinson, C. (eds.) (2004) *Doing Research with Children and Young People*, London: Sage

Fraser, S., Maher, J. and Wright, J. (2010) 'Between Bodies and Collectivities: Articulating the Action of Emotion in Obesity Epidemic Discourse' *Social Theory & Health*, vol.8(2), 192–209

Freund, P. E. (1990) 'The Expressive Body: A Common Ground for the Sociology of Emotions and Health and Illness' *Sociology of Health and Illness*, vol.12(4), 453–477

Friedlander, M. L. (2003) 'Adoption: Misunderstood, Mythologized, Marginalised' *The Counseling Psychologist*, vol.31(6), 745–752

Gaber, I. and Aldridge, J. (1994) Introduction, in Gaber, I. and Aldridge, J. (eds.) *In The Best Interests of the Child Culture, Identity and Transracial Adoption*, London: Free Association Books, 1–5

Gailey, C. W. (2000) Race, Class and Gender in Intercountry Adoption in the USA, in Selman, P. (ed) *Intercountry Adoption Developments, Trends and Perspectives*, London: BAAF Publications, 295–313

Gallacher, L. (2005) 'The Terrible Twos: Gaining Control in the Nursery?' *Children's Geographies*, vol.3(2), 243–246

Gallacher, L. and Gallagher, M. (2008) 'Methodological Immaturity in Childhood Research? Thinking through Participatory Methods' *Childhood*, vol.15(4), 499–516

Garfinkel, H. (1967) *Studies in Ethnomethodology*, New Jersey: Prentice-Hall

Garrett, P. M. (2009) *Transforming Children's Services? Social Work, Neoliberalism and the Modern World*, Maidenhead: Open University Press

Giddens, A. (1979) *Action, Structure and Contradiction in Social Analysis*, Berkeley, CA: University of California Press

Giddens, A. (1984) *The Constitution of Society*, Cambridge: Polity Press

Giddens, A. (1991a) *Modernity and Self-Identity: Self and Society in the Late Modern Age*, Cambridge: Polity Press

Giddens, A. (1991b) *The Consequences of Modernity*, Cambridge: Polity Press

Giddens, A. (1993) *New Rules of Sociological Method: A Positive Critique of Interpretive Sociologies* (2nd ed.), Cambridge: Polity Press

Gilligan, C. (1993) *In a Different Voice* (2nd ed.), London: Harvard University Press

Gilligan, T. (2014) 'Paedophilia Is Natural and Normal for Males: How Some University Academics Make the Case for Paedophiles at Summer Conferences' *The Telegraph*, 5th July

Goffman, E. (1959) *The Presentation of Self in Everyday Life*, London: Penguin

Goode, S. (2010) *Understanding and Addressing Adult Sexual Attraction to Children*, Abingdon: Routledge

Graue, E. M. and Walsh, D. J. (1998) *Studying Children in Social Context: Theories, Methods and Ethics*, London: Sage

Greenfield, P. M. (1994) Independence and Interdependence as Developmental Scripts; Implications for Theory, Research and Practice, in Greenfield, P. M. and Cocking, R. R. (eds.) *Cross-Cultural Roots of Minority Child Development*, New Jersey: Erloaum, 1–37

Greig, A., Taylor, J. and Mackay, T. (2013) *Doing Research with Children a Practical Guide* (3rd ed.), London: Sage

Griffith, A. (1998) 'Insider/Outsider: Epistemological Privilege and Mothering Work' *Human Studies*, vol.21, 361–376

Guba, E. G. and Lincoln, Y. S. (1994) Competing Paradigms in Qualitative Research, in Denzin, N. K. and Lincoln, Y. S. (eds.) *Handbook of Qualitative Research*, Thousand Oaks, CA: Sage, 105–117

Guillemin, M. and Gillam, L. (2004) 'Ethics, Reflexivity, and "Ethically Important Moments" in Research' *Qualitative Inquiry*, vol.10(2), 261–280

Guta, A., Nixon, S. A. and Wilson, M. G. (2013) 'Resisting the Seduction of "Ethics Creep": Using Foucault to Surface Complexity and Contradiction in Research Ethics Review' *Social Science and Medicine*, vol.98, 301–310

Haavind, H. (2005) 'Review Essay Towards a Multifaceted Understanding of Children as Social Participants' *Childhood*, vol.12(1), 139–152

Hacking, I. (1986) Making Up People, in Heller, P., Sosna, M. and Wellbery, D. (eds.) *Reconstructing Individualism*, Stanford: Stanford University Press, 222–236

Hallowell, N., Lawton, J. and Gregory, S. (2005) *Reflections on Research: The Realities of Doing Research in the Social Sciences*, Buckingham: Open University Press

Hammersley, M. (2009) 'Against the Ethicists: On the Evils of Ethical Regulation' *International Journal of Social Research Methodology*, vol.12(3), 211–225

Hammersley, M. and Atkinson, P. (1995) *Ethnography Principles in Practice* (2nd ed.), London: Routledge

Hammersley, M. and Traianou, A. (2011) 'Moralism and Research Ethics: A Machiavellian Perspective' *International Journal of Social Research Methodology*, vol.14(5), 379–390

Hammersley, M. and Traianou, A. (2012) *Ethics in Qualitative Research: Controversies and Contexts*, London: Sage

Haraway, D. (1991) *Simians, Cyborgs and Women* New York: Routledge and Kegan Paul

Harden, J., Scott, S., Backett-Milburn, K. and Jackson, S. (2000) 'Can't talk, Won't Talk? Methodological Issues in Researching Children' *Sociological Research Online*, 5(2), Available at: http://www.socresonline.org.uk/5/2/harden.html [Accessed: 20th June 2013]

Harden, J. (2012) 'Good Sitting, Looking and Listening: The Regulation of Young Children's Emotions in the Classroom' *Children's Geographies*, vol.10(1), 83–93

Harris, A. (2003) 'gURL Scenes and grrrl zines: The Regulation and Resistance of Girls in Late Modernity' *Feminist Review*, vol.75, 38–56

Hartsock, N. (1996) 'Postmodernism and Political Change: Issues for Feminist Theory', in Hekman, S. J. (ed) *Feminist Interpretations of Michel Foucault*, Pennsylvania: Pennsylvania State University Press, 39–58

Haugen, G. M. D. (2008) 'Children's Perspectives on Everyday Experiences of Shared Residence: Time, Emotions and Agency Dilemmas' *Children in Society*, vol.11, 71–94

Heath, S., Charles, V., Crow, G. and Wiles, R., (2007) 'Informed Consent, Gatekeepers and Go-Betweens: Negotiating Consent in Child and Youth-Orientated Institutions' *British Educational Research Journal*, vol.33(3), 403–417

Hendrick, H. (2000) The Child as Social Actor in Historical Sources. Problems of Identification and Interpretation, in Christensen, P. and James, A. (eds.) *Research with Children: Perspectives and Practices*, London: Falmer Press, 36–61

Hendrick, H. (ed) (2005) *Child Welfare and Social Policy*, Bristol: Policy Press

Heritage, John (1984) *Garfinkel and Ethnomethodology*, Cambridge: Polity Press

Herz, R. (1996) 'Introduction: Ethics, Reflexivity and Voice' *Qualitative Sociology*, vol.19(1), 3–9

Hester, S. and Eglin, P. (1997) *Culture in Action: Studies in Membership Categorisation Analysis*, Washington: University Press of America

Hewson, C., Yule, P., Laurent, D. and Vogel, C. (2003). *Internet Research Methods: A Practical Guide for the Behavioural and Social Sciences*, London: Sage

Hill, E. J. (2005) 'Work-Family Facilitation and Conflict, Working Fathers and Mothers, Work-Family Stressors and Support' *Journal of Family Issues*, 26(6), 793–819

Hine C. (2005) 'Internet Research and the Sociology of Cyber-Social-Scientific Knowledge' *Information Society*, 21(4), 239–248

Hobbs, D. and May, T. (1993) *Interpreting the Field: Accounts of Ethnography*, Oxford: Clarendon Press

Hochschild, A. (1983) *The Managed Heart: Commercialization of Human Feeling*, Berkeley: University of California Press

Hockey, J. and James, A. (1993) *Growing Up and Growing Old: Ageing and Dependency in the Life Course*, London: Sage

Högbacka, R. (2012) Maternal Thinking in the Context of Stratified Reproduction: Perspectives of Birth Mothers from South Africa, in Gibbons, J. L. and Rotabi, K. S. (eds.) *Intercountry Adoption, Policies, Practices and Outcomes*, Surrey: Ashgate, 143–159

Holland, P. (1992) *What Is a Child?: Popular Images of Childhood*, London: Virago

Hollway, W. and Jefferson, T. (2000) *Doing Qualitative Research Differently: Free Association, Narrative and the Interview Method*, London: Sage

Holloway, S. and Valentine, G. (eds.) (2000) *Children's Geographies: Playing, Living, Learning*, London: Routledge

Holloway, S. and Valentine, G. (2001) ' "It's Only as Stupid as you are": Children's and Adult's Negotiation of ICT Competence at Home and at School' *Social and Cultural Geography*, vol.2(1), 25–42

Holmes, J. (1997) 'Women, Language, Identity' *Journal of Sociolinguistics*, vol.1(2), 195–223

Holstein, J. A. and Gubrium, J. F. (1995) *The Active Interview* Thousand Oaks, CA: Sage

Howarth, C. (2002) 'Using the Theory of Social Representation to Explore Difference in the Research Relationship' *Qualitative Research*, vol.2(1), 21–34

Hudson, J. M. and Bruckman, A. (2004) ' "Go away": Participant Objections to Being Studied and the Ethics of Chat Room Research' *The Information Society*, vol.20, 127–139

Huxley, P., Evans, S., Davidson, B. and King, S. (2005) 'The Costs of Scrutiny in Applied Health and Social Care Research: A Case Study' *Research Policy and Planning*, vol.23(1), 55–60

Hydén, M. (2008) Narrating Sensitive Topics, in Squire, C., Andrews, M. and Tamboukou, M. (eds.) *Doing Narrative Research*, London: Sage, 121–127

Jackson, A. Y. (2003) 'Rhizovocality' *Qualitative Studies in Education*, vol.16(5), 693–710

Jacobson, H. (2008) *Culture Keeping*, Nashville: Vanderbilt University Press

James, A. and James, A. (2004) *Constructing Childhood*, Basingstoke: Palgrave Macmillan

James, A., Jenks, C. and Prout, A. (1998) *Theorising Childhood*, Cambridge: Polity Press

James, A. and Prout, A. (1997) Re-Presenting Childhood: Time and Transition in the Study of Childhood, in James, A. and Prout, A. (eds.) *Constructing and Reconstructing Childhood*, London: Falmer Press, 230–250

Jayyusi, L. (1984) *Categorization and the Moral Order*, London: Routledge and Kegan Paul

Jenks, C. (1996) *Childhood*, London: Routledge

Jenks, C. (2005) 'Journeys into Space' *Childhood*, vol.12(4), 419–424

Johnson, K. (2012) Challenging the Discourse of Intercountry Adoption: Perspectives from Rural China, in Gibbons, J. L. and Rotabi, K. S. (eds.) *Intercountry Adoption Policies, Practices, and Outcomes*, Farnham: Ashgate, 103–117

Jordan, A. B. (2006) 'Make Yourself at Home: The Social Construction of Research Roles in Family Studies' *Qualitative Research*, vol.6(2), 169–185

Kanuka, H. and Anderson, T. (2007). 'Ethical Issues in Qualitative E-learning Research' *International Journal of Qualitative Methods*, 6(2), Available at: http://www.ualberta.ca/~iiqm/backissues/6_2/kanuka.htm [Accessed: 20th May 2015]

Kehily, M. J. (2012) 'Contextualising the Sexualisation of Girls Debate: Innocence, Experience and Young Female Sexuality' *Gender and Education*, vol.24(3), 255–268

Kellet, M. (2005) *How to Develop Children as Researchers*, London: Paul Chapman Publishing

Kellett, M., Robinson, C. and Burr, R. (2004) Images of Childhood, in Fraser, S., Lewis, V., Ding, S., Kellet, M. and Robinson, C. (eds.) *Doing Research with Children and Young People*, London: Sage, 161–174

Killen, M. and Wainryb, C. (2000) Independence and Interdependence in Diverse Cultural Contexts, in Harkness, S. and Raeff, C. (eds.) *Individualism and Collectivism as Cultural Contexts for Development*, San Francisco: Jossey-Bass, 5–22

Kirschner, D. (1990) 'The Adopted Child Syndrome: Considerations for Psychotherapy' *Psychotherapy in Private Practice*, vol.8(3), 93–100

Kirton, D. (1996) 'Race and Adoption' *Critical Social Policy*, vol.46(16), 123–136

Kitchin, R. (2000) 'The Researched Opinions on Research: Disabled People and Disability Research' *Disability and Society*, vol.15(1), 25–47

Krieger, S. (1987) 'Beyond Subjectivity: The Use of the Self in Social Science' *Qualitative Sociology*, vol.8(4), 309–324

Komulainen, S. (2007) 'The Ambiguity of the Child's "Voice" in Social Research' *Childhood*, vol.14(1), 11–28

Lahman, M. K. E. (2008) 'Always Othered: Ethical Research with Children' *Journal of Early Childhood Research*, vol.6(3), 281–300

Laidlaw, J. (2014) The Undefined Work of Freedom: Foucault's Genealogy and the Anthropology of Ethics, in Faubion, J. D. (ed) *Foucault Now*, Cambridge: Polity, 23–37

Lange, A. and Mierendorff, J. (2009) Method and Methodology in Childhood Research, in Qvortrup, J., Corsaro, W. and Honig, M. (eds.) *The Palgrave Handbook of Childhood Studies*, Basingstoke: Palgrave Macmillan, 78–95

Lansdown, G. (1994) Children's Rights, in Mayall, B. (ed) *Children's Childhoods Experienced and Observed*, London: Falmer Press, 33–42

Lawler, S. (2008) Stories in the Social World, in Pickering, M. (ed) *Research in Cultural Studies*, Edinburgh: Edinburgh University Press, 32–49

Lawler, S. (2014) *Identity Sociological Perspectives* (2nd ed.), Cambridge: Polity

Lee, N. (1999) 'The Challenge of Childhood; Distributions of Childhood's Ambiguity in Adult Institutions' *Childhood*, vol.6(4), 455–474

Leicester, M. (1999) *Disability Voice-Towards an Enabling Education*, London: Jessica Kingsley Publishers

Leinaweaver, J. B. (2008) *The Circulation of Children Kinship, Adoption, and Morality in Andean Peru*, Durham: Duke University Press

Lewis, M. (2001) *Learning to Listen: Consulting Children and Young People with Disabilities*, London: Save the Children

Lewis, A. (2008) 'Silence in the Context of "Child Voice" ' *Children and Society*, vol.24, 14–23

Lewis, A. (2010) 'Silence in the Context of "Child Voice" ' *Children & Society*, vol.24(1), 14–23

Lewis, V., Kellett, M., Robinson, C., Fraser, S. and Ding, S. (2004) *The Reality of Research with Children and Young People*, London: Sage

Lewis, A. and Porter, J. (2004) 'Interviewing Children and Young People with Learning Disabilities: Guidelines for Researchers and Multi-Professional Practice' *British Journal of Learning Disabilities*, vol.32, 191–197

Livingstone, S. M. (2002) *Young People and New Media: Childhood and the Changing Media Environment*, London: Sage

Livingstone, S. (2006) Children's Privacy Online: Experimenting with Boundaries Within and Beyond the Family, in Kraut, R., Brynin, M. and Kiesler, S. (eds.) *Computers, Phones, and the Internet: Domesticating Information Technology*, Oxford: Oxford University Press, 145–167

Livingstone, S. (2008) 'Taking Risky Opportunities in Youthful Content Creation: Teenagers' Use of Social Networking Sites for Intimacy, Privacy and Self-expression' *New Media & Society*, vol.10(3), 393–411

Livingstone, S. and Haddon, L. (2009) EU Kids Online: Final Report. Deliverable D6.5 for the EC Safer Internet plus programme, Available at: http://eprints.lse.ac.uk/24372/ [Accessed: 9th Jan 2015]

Lloyd Smith, M. and Tarr, J. (2000) Researching Children's Perspectives: A Sociological Dimension, in Lewis, A. and Lindsay, G. (eds.) *Researching Children's Perspectives*, Buckingham: Open University Press, 59–70

Luff, D. (1999) 'Doing Social Research: Issues and Dilemmas' *Sociology*, vol.33(4), 687–703

Lukes, S. (2005) *Power: A Radical View*, Basingstoke: Palgrave Macmillan

Lull, J. (1985) Ethnographic Studies of Broadcast Media Audiences, in Dominick, J. and Fletcher, J. (eds.) *Broadcasting Research Methods*, Boston, MA: Allyn & Bacon, 80–87

Mackenzie, C. and Stoljar, N. (eds.) (2000) *Relational Autonomy: Feminist Perspectives on Autonomy, Agency and the Social Self*, Oxford: Oxford University Press

MacNaughton, G., Hughes, P. and Smith, K. (2007) 'Young Children's Rights and Public Policy: Practices and Possibilities for Citizenship in the Early Years' *Children and Society*, vol.21, 458–469

Madden, R. (2010) *Being Ethnographic A Guide to the Theory and Practice of Ethnography*, London: Sage

Madge, C. (2007) 'Developing a Geographers Agenda for Online Research Ethics' *Progress in Human Geography*, vol.31, 654–674

Madison, D. S. (1988) Performance, Personal Narratives, and the Politics of Possibility', in Dailey, S. J. (ed) *The Future of Performance Studies: Visions and Revisions*, Washington: National Communication Association, 276–286

Madison, D. S. (2005) *Critical Ethnography Method, Ethics and Performance*, London: Sage

Mahon, A., Glendinning, C., Clarke, K. and Craig, G. (1996) 'Researching Children: Methods and Ethics' *Children and Society*, vol.10, 145–154

Malaguzzi, L. (1993) History, Ideas and Basic Philosophy: An Interview with Lella Gandini, in Edwards, C., Gandini, L. and Foreman, G. (eds.) *The Hundred Languages of Children: Reggio Emilia Approach – Advanced Reflections*, Greenwich: Alex Publishing Corporation, 49–98

Mandelbaum, J. (1978) 'Assigning Responsibility in Conversational Storytelling: The Interactional Construction of Reality' *Text*, vol.13(2), 247–266

Mandell, N. (1991) The Least Adult Role in Studying Children, in Waksler, F. C. (ed) *Studying the Social Worlds of Children: Sociological Readings*, London: Falmer Press, 38–59

Mann, C. and Stewart, F. (2000) *Internet Communication and Qualiltative Research: A Handbook for Researching Online*, London: Sage

Marchant, R. and Crisp, A. (2001) *What We Think: Views of Children and Young People in Southwark*, Brighton: Triangle

Masson, J. (2000) Researching Children's Perspectives: Legal Issues, in Lewis, A. and Lindsay, G. (eds.) *Researching Children's Perspectives*, Buckingham: Open University Press, 34–45

Mauthner, M., Birch. M., Jessop, J. and Miller, T. (2002) *Ethics in Qualitative Research*, London: Sage

Mauthner, N. S. and Doucet, A. (2003) 'Reflexive Accounts and Accounts of Reflexivity in Qualitative Data Analysis' *Sociology*, vol.37(3), 413–431

Mayall, B. (2000a) Conversations with Children: Working with Generational Issues, in Christensen, P. and James, A. (eds.) *Advocating for Children: International Perspectives on Children's Rights*, London: Falmer Press, 120–135

Mayall, B. (2000b) Conversations with Children: Working with Generational Issues, in Christensen, P. and James, A. (eds.) *Research with Children: Perspectives and Practices*, London: Routledge, 109–124

Mayall, B. (2002) *Towards a Sociology of Childhood. Thinking from Children's Lives*, Maidenhead: Open University Press

Mayall, B. (2008) Conversations with Children: Working with Generational Issues, in Christensen, P. and James, A. (eds.) *Research with Children: Perspectives and Practices*, (2nd ed.), London, Routledge Falmer, 109–122

McDowell, L., Ray, K., Perrons, D., Pagan, C. and Ward, K. (2005) 'Women's Paid Work and Moral Economies of Care' *Social and Cultural Geography*, vol.6, 219–235

McKie, L. and Callan, S. (2012) *Understanding Families*, London: Sage

Mead, G. H. (1974) *Mind, Self and Society* (2nd ed.), Chicago: University of Chicago Press

Miller, S. (2000) 'Researching Children: Issues Arising from a Phenomenological Study with Children Who Have Diabetes Mellitus' *Journal of Advanced Nursing*, vol.31, 1228–1234

Miller, J. and Glassner, B. (1997) The "Inside" and the "Outside": Finding Realities in Interviews, in Silverman, D. (ed) *Qualitative Research; Theory, Method and Practice*, London: Sage, 99–112

Mishler, E. G. (1986) *Research Interviewing: Context and Narrative*, Cambridge, MA: Harvard University Press

Moeller, S. (1998) *Compassion Fatigue: How the Media Sell Disease, Famine, War and Death*, New York: Routledge

Monaghan, L., O'Dwyer, M. and Gabe, J. (2012) 'Seeking University Research Ethics Committee approval: The Emotional Vicissitudes of a "Rationalised" Process' *International Journal of Social Research Methodology*, vol.16(1), 65–80

Montgomery, H. (2007) 'Working with Child Prostitutes in Thailand: Problems of Practice and Interpretation' *Childhood*, vol.14(4), 415–430

Morris, J. (1998) *The Experiences of Disabled Children and Young People Living Away from Their Families*, London: The Who Cares? Trust

Morris, J. (2003) 'Including all Children. Finding out the Experiences of Children with Communication and/or Cognitive Impairments' *Children and Society*, vol.17(5), 337–348

Morris, L. (2006) A Foundation for Rights or Theories of Practice?, in Morris, L. (ed) *Rights: Sociological Perspectives*, London: Routledge, 240–252

Mullin, A. (2014) 'Children, Paternalism and the Development of Autonomy' *Ethic Theory Moral Practice*, vol.17, 413–426

Murphy, E. (n.d.) *Images of Childhood in Mothers Accounts of Childrearing*, Nottingham University, Available at: http://eprints.nottingham.ac.uk/775/1/Images_of_Childhood_in_Mothers'_Accounts_of_Contemporary_Childrearing.pdf [Accessed: 30th July 2012]

Noelle-Neuman, E. (1984) *The Spiral of Silence: Public Opinion, Our Social Skin*, Chicago: University of Chicago Press

Oakley, A. (1981) Interviewing Women: A Contradiction in Terms, in Roberts, H. (ed) *Doing Feminist Research*, London: Routledge, 30–61

Oakley, A. (2007) *Fracture: Adventures of a Broken Body*, Bristol: The Policy Press

Oliver, M. (1992) 'Changing the Social Relations of Research Production' *Disability, Handicap and Society*, vol.7, 101–114

Oliver, M. (1996) *Understanding Disability: From Theory to Practice*, Basingstoke: Macmillan

Papacharissi, Z. (2009) 'The Virtual Geographies of Social Networks: A Comparative Analysis of Facebook, LinkedIn and ASmallWorld' *New Media and Society*, vol.11(1–2), 199–220

Parnell, R. and Patsarika, M. (2011) 'Young People's Participation in School Design: Exploring Diversity and Power in a UK Governmental Policy-Case Study' *Children's Geographies*, vol.9(3–4), 457–475

Parry, G. (1991) Conclusion: Paths to Citizenship, in Vogel, U. and Moran, M. (eds.) *Frontiers of Citizenship*, London: Macmillan, 166–201

Parton, N. (2006) ' "Every Child Matters" the Shift to Prevention Whilst Strengthening Protection in Children's Services in England' *Children & Youth Services Review*, vol.28(2), 976–992

Patai, D. (1991) U.S. Academics and Third World Women: Is Ethical Research Possible?, in Gluck, S. B. and Patai, D. (eds.) *Women's Words: The Feminist Practice of Oral History*, New York: Routledge and Kegan Paul

Paterson, K. and Hughes, B. (1999) 'Disability Studies and Phenomenology: The Carnal Politics of Everyday Life' *Disability and Society*, vol.14(5), 597–611

Phoenix, A. (2008) Analysing Narrative Contexts, in Andrews, M., Squire, C. and Tamboukou, M. (eds.) *Doing Narrative Research*, London: Sage, 64–78

Pike, J. (2008) 'Foucault, Space and the Primary School Dining Room' *Children's Geographies*, vol.6(4), 413–422

Pink, S. (2012) *Situating Everyday Life*, London: Sage

Pittenger, D. (2003) 'Internet Research: An Opportunity to Revisit Classic Ethical Problems in Behavioural Research' *Ethics and Behaviour*, vol.13(1), 45–60

Plummer, K. (2001) *Documents of Life 2: An Invitation to Critical Humanism* (2nd ed.), London: Sage

Poindexter, C. C. (2003) 'The Ubiquity of Ambiguity in Research Interviewing: An Exemplar' *Qualitative Social Work*, vol.2(4), 383–409

Pole, C. (2007) 'Researching Children and Fashion: An Embodied Ethnography' *Childhood*, vol.14(1), 67–84

Potter, J. (1996) *Representing Reality: Discourse, Rhetoric and Social Construction*, London: Sage

Potter, J. and Wetherell, M. (1987) *Discourse and Social Psychology: Beyond Attitudes and Behaviour*, London: Sage

Potter, C. and Whittaker, C. (2001) *Enabling Communication in Children with Autism*, London: Jessica Kingsley

Powell, M. A. and Smith, A. B. (2010) 'Ethical Guidelines for Research with Children: A Review of Current Research Documentation in New Zealand' *Kotuitui: New Zealand Journal of Social Sciences Online*, vol.1(2), 125–138

Prentsky, M. (2001) 'Digital Natives, Digital Immigrants Part 1' *On the Horizon*, vol.9(5), 1–6

Priestly, M. (1998a) 'Childhood, Disability and Disabled Childhoods – Agendas for Research' *Childhood – A Global Journal of Child Research*, vol.5(2), 207–223

Priestley, M. (1998) 'Constructions and Creations: Idealism, Materialism and Disability Theory' *Disability and Society*, vol.13(1), 75–94

Prout, A. (2005) *The Future of Childhood*, London: Falmer Press

Prout, A. and Hallett, C. (2003) Introduction, in Prout, A. and Hallett, C. (eds.) *Hearing the Voices of Children: Social Policy for a New Century*, London: Routledge Falmer, 1–8

Punch, S. (2002) 'Research with Children: The Same or Different from Research with Adults?' *Childhood*, vol.9(3), 321–341

Qvortrup, J., Bardy, M., Sgritta, G. and Wintersberger, H. (eds.) (1994) *Childhood Matters*, Aldershot: Avebury

Rabiee, P., Sloper, P. and Beresford, B. (2005) 'Desired Outcomes for Children and Young People with Complex Health Care Needs, and Children Who Do Not Use Speech for Communication' *Health and Social Care in the Community*, vol.13(5), 478–487

Reinharz. S. (1979) *On Becoming a Social Scientist*, San Francisco: Jossey-Bass

Riessman, C. K. (1994) 'Subjectivity Matters: The Positioned Investigator', in Riessman, C. K. (ed) *Qualitative Studies in Social Work Research*, Thousand Oaks: Sage, 139–52

Richards, S. (2012a) ' "Why are we not Allowed to Comfort Children when they've been Told off?": The Social Positioning of Children and Their Capacity for Ethical Agency' *Childhood Remixed*, vol.1, 48–54, University Campus Suffolk

Richards, S. (2012b) What the Map Cuts up the Story Cuts Across: Narratives of Belonging in Intercountry Adoption, in Simmonds, J. and Phoenix, A. (eds.) *Multiculturalism, Identity and Family Placement*, in Adoption & Fostering, vol.36(3–4), 104–111

Richards, S. (2013) 'Stories of Paper and Blood: Narratives of Belonging in Families with Daughters Adopted from China'. PhD dissertation, Institute of Education, University of London

Richards, S. (2014) 'HCIA Implementation and the Best Interests of the Child' *ISS Working Paper Series/General Series*, vol.597, 1–18. International Institute of Social Studies of Erasmus University (ISS). Retrieved from http://hdl.handle.net/1765/77407

Ricoeur, P. (1991) *From Text to Action*, Illinois: Northwestern University Press

Ringrose, J. (2011) Beyond Discourse? Using Deleuze and Guattari's Schizoanalysis to Explore Affective Assemblages, Heterosexually Striated Space and Lines of Flight Online and at School, *Educational Philosophy and Theory*, vol.43(6), 598–618

Ringrose, J. and Eriksson Barajas, K. (2011) Gendered Risks and Opportunities? Exploring Teen Girls' Digital Sexual Identity in Post Feminist Media Contexts, *International Journal of Media and Cultural Politics*, vol.7(2), 121–138

Richman, A. (2007) The Outsider Lurking Online; Adults Researching Youth Cybercultures, in Best, A. L. (ed) *Representing Youth: Methodological Issues in Critical Youth Studies*, New York: New York University Press, 182–202

Ristock, J. L. and Pennell, J. (1996) *Community Research as Empowerment: Feminist Links, Postmodern Interpretations*, Toronto: Oxford University Press

Robinson, K. (2013) *Innocence, Knowledge and the Construction of Childhood: The Contradictory Nature of Sexuality and Censorship in Children's Contemporary Lives*, London: Routledge

Rodgers, J. (1999) 'Trying to Get It Right: Undertaking Research Involving People with Learning Difficulties' *Disability and Society*, vol.14(4), 421–433

Rojiani, R. H. (1994) Disparities in the Social Construction of Long-Term Care, in Riessman, C. K. (ed) *Qualitative Studies in Social Work*, California: Sage, 139–152

Rose, N. (1999) *Powers of Freedom: Reframing Political Thought*, Cambridge: Cambridge University Press

Roseneil, S. (1993) Greenham Revisited: Researching Myself and My Sisters, in Hobbs, D. and May, T. (eds.) *Interpreting the Field: Accounts of Ethnography*, Oxford: Clarendon Press, 177–208

Sacks, H. (1974) An Analysis of the Course of a Joke's Telling in Conversation, in Bauman, R. and Sherzer, J. F. (eds.) *Explorations in the Ethnography of Speaking*, Cambridge: Cambridge University Press, 337–353

Sacks, H. (1992) Lectures on Conversation, Volumes I and II, in by Jefferson, G., with Introduction by Schegloff, E. A., Oxford: Blackwell

Sandbaek, M. (1999) 'Adult Images of Childhood and Research on Client Children' *International Journal of Social Research Methodology*, vol.2, 191–202

Saunders, J. S. (2008) 'Spinning Sympathy: Orphan Girl Novels and the Sentimental Tradition' *Children's Literature Association Quarterly*, vol.33(1), 41–62

Scott, J. (2000) Children as Respondents: The Challenge for Quantitative Methods, in Christensen, P. and James, A. (eds.) *Research with Children: Perspectives and Practices*, London: Falmer Press, 36–61

Schutz, A. (1962) 'Choosing Among Projects of Action', in Natanson, M. (ed) *Collected Papers*, vol.1 *The Problem of Social Reality*, The Hague: Martinus Nijhoff, 67–94

Segal, L. (1999) *Why Feminism? Gender, Psychology, Politics*, Cambridge: Polity

Shah, S. (2006) 'Sharing the World: The Researcher and the Researched' *Qualitative Research*, vol.6(2), 207–220

Shakespeare, T. (1996) Disability, Identity, Difference, in Barnes, C. and Mercer, G. (eds.) *Exploring the Divide; Illness and Disability*, Leeds: Disability Press, 94–113

Shakespeare, T. (2000) *Help*, Birmingham: Venture Press

Shakespeare, T. (2006) *Disability Rights and Wrongs*, Oxon: Routledge

Short, G. (1999) Children's Grasp of Controversial Issues, in Woodhead, M., Faulkner, D. and Littleton, K. (eds.) *Making Sense of Social Development*, London: Routledge, 153–169

Sieber, J. and Stanley, B. (1988) 'Ethical and Professional Dimensions of Socially Sensitive Research' *American Psychologist*, vol.42, 49–55

Sikes, P. and Piper, H. (2010) 'Ethical Research, Academic Freedom and the Role of Ethics Committees and Review Procedures in Educational Research'

*International Journal of Research and Method in Education, Special Issue: Ethics and Academic Freedom in Educational Research*, vol.33(3), 205–213

Silverman, D. and Gubrium, J. (1989) Introduction, in Silverman, D. and Gubrium, J. (eds.) *The Politics of Field Research: Sociology Beyond Enlightenment*, London: Sage, 1–13

Simons, K., Booth, T. and Booth, W. (1989) 'Speaking Out: User Studies and People with Learning Disabilities' *Advances in Psychiatric Treatment*, vol.1, 207–213

Simons, H. and Usher, R. (2002) *Situated Ethics in Educational Research*, New York: Routledge

Sin, C. H. (2005) 'Seeking Informed Consent: Reflections on Research Practice' *Sociology*, vol.39(2), 277–294

Skelton, T. (2008) 'Research with Children and Young Children: Exploring the Tensions Between Ethics, Competence and Participation' *Children's Geographies*, vol.6(1), 21–36

Shah, S. (2006) 'Sharing the World: The Researcher and the Researched' *Qualitative Research*, vol.6(2), 207–220

Silverman, D. (1993) *'Beginning Research'. Interpreting Qualitative Data. Methods for Analysing Talk, Text and Interaction*, London: Sage

Silverman, D. (1998) *Harvey Sacks: Social Science & Conversation Analysis*, Cambridge: polity Press

Slote, M. (2007) *The Ethics of Care and Empathy*, Abingdon: Routledge

Smart, C., Neale, B. and Wade, A. (2001) *The Changing Experience of Childhood: Families and Divorce*, Cambridge: Polity Press

Smith, F. and Barker, J. (2000) 'Contested Spaces: Children's Experiences of out of School Care in England and Wales' *Childhood*, vol.7(3), 315–333

Smith, Mark J. (2005) *Reinventing the Social Sciences: Towards a Post Disciplinary Future*, London, UK: Sage Publications

Smolin, D. M. (2006) 'Child Laundering: How the Intercountry Adoption System Legitimizes and Incentivizes the Practices of Buying, Trafficking, Kidnapping, and Stealing Children' *Wayne Law Review*, vol.52(1), 113–200, Available at: http://wors.bepress.com/david_smolin/1 [Accessed: 9th January 2015]

Smyres, K. (1999) 'Virtual Corporeality: Adolescent Girls and their Bodies in Cyberspace' *Research Methodology Online*, Available at: http://www.socio.demon.co.uk/magazine/6/smyres.html [Accessed: 21st May 2015]

Song, M. and Parker, D. (1995) 'Commonality, Difference and the Dynamics of Disclosure in In-Depth Interviewing' *Sociology*, vol.29(2), 241–256

Spriggs, M. (2010) *Understanding Consent in Research Involving Children: The Ethical Issues*, The Royal Children's Hospital, Melbourne, Available at: www.mori.edu.au/media/62539/handbook.pdf [Accessed: 9th January 2015]

Spyrou, S. (2011) 'The Limits to Children's Voices: From Authenticity to Critical Reflexive Representation' *Childhood*, vol.18(2), 151–165

Stacey, J. (1996) Can There Be a Feminist Ethnography?, in Gottfried, H. (ed) *Feminism and Social Change: Bridging Theory and Practice*, Illinois: University of Illinois Press, 88–101

Stainton Rogers, W. (2001) Constructing Childhood: Constructing Child Concern, in Foley, P., Roche, J. and Tucker, S. (eds.), *Childhood in Society: Contemporary Theory, Policy and Practice*, London: Basingstoke, 26–33

Stalker, K. (2012) 'Researching the Lives of Disabled Children' *Children and Society*, vol.26, 173–180

Stalker, K. and Connors, C. (2003) 'Communicating with Disabled Children' *Adoption and Fostering*, vol.27(1), 26–35

Stanley, L. and Wise, S. (1993) *Breaking Out Again: Feminist Ontology and Epistemology*, London: Routledge

Stanley, L. and Wise, S. (2010) 'The ESRC's 2010 Framework for Ethics: Fit for Research Purpose?' *Sociological Research Online*, 15(4), 12, Available at http://www.socresonline.org.uk/15/4/12.html

Stern, S. (2004) Studying Adolescents Online: A Consideration of Ethical Issues, in Buchanan, E. (ed) *Readings in Virtual Research Ethics: Issues and Controversies*, Hershey, PA: Ideal Group, 274–287

Stones, R. (2005) *Structuration Theory*, Basingstoke: Palgrave MacMillan

Strauss, A. L. (1977) *Mirrors and Masks: The Search for Identity*, New Jersey: Transaction Publishers

Tapscott, D. (1998) *Growing Up Digital. The Rise of the Net Generation*, New York: McGraw Hill

Taylor, L. (1998) 'Confidentiality: Competing Principles, Inevitable Dilemmas' *Journal of Education and Psychological Consultation*, vol.9(3), 267–275

Taylor, J. (2011) 'The Intimate Insider: Negotiating the Ethics of Friendship when Doing Insider Research' *Qualitative Research*, vol.11(3), 3–22

The National Children's Bureau (2003) Guidelines for Research, Available at: www.ncb.org.uk/research/research guidelines.pdf [Accessed: 21st August 2013]

Thomas, N. and O'Kane, C. (1998) 'The Ethics of Participatory Research with Children' *Children and Society*, vol.12, 336–348

Thomas, N. and O'Kane, C. (2000) 'Discovering What Children Think: Connections Between Research and Practice' *British Journal of Social Work*, vol.30, 819–835

Thorne, B. (1980) ' "You Still Takin' Notes?" Fieldwork and Problems of Informed Consent' *Social Problems*, vol.27(3), 284–297

Thornton, S. (1995) *Club Cultures: Music, Media and Subcultural Capital* Oxford: Polity

Tilly, C. (1994) 'History and Sociological Imagining' *Tocqueville Review*, vol.15, 57–74

Triseliotis, J. P., Shireman, J. F. and Hundleby, M. (1997) *Adoption: Theory, Policy and Practice*, London: Cassel

Tronto, J. C. (2009) *Moral Boundaries a Political Argument for an Ethic of Care*, New York: Routledge

Twine, F. (1994) *Citizenship and Social Rights*, London: Sage

Twycross, A. (2009) 'An Interprofessional Approach to the Ethics of Undertaking Research with Children' *Nurse Researcher*, vol.16(3), 7–20

United Nations (1989) *Conventions on the Rights of the Child*, United Nations: Geneva

Uprichard, E. (2008) 'Children as Being and Becoming: Children, Childhood and Temporality' *Children and Society*, vol.22(4), 303–313

Uprichard, E. (2010) 'Questioning Research with Children: Discrepancy Between Theory and Practice?' *Children & Society*, vol.24(1), 3–13

Veale, A. (2005) Creative Methodologies in Participatory Research with Children, in Greene, S. and Hogan, D. (eds.) *Researching Children's Experience*, London: Sage, 253–269

Walkerdine, V. (1989) 'Femininity as Performance' *Oxford Review of Education*, vol.15 (3), 267–279

Walkerdine, V. (1999) 'Violent Boys and Precocious Girls: Regulating Childhood at the End of the Millennium' *Contemporary Issues in Early Childhood*, vol.1(1), 3–23

Wall, L. (2010) *Ethics in Light of Childhood*, Washington: Georgetown University Press

Waller, T. (2010) ' "Let's Throw that Big Stick in the River": An Exploration of Gender in the Construction of Shared Narratives around Outdoor Spaces' *European Early Childhood Education Research*, vol.18(4), 527–542

Waller, T. and Bitou, A. (2011) 'Research with Children: Three Challenges for Participatory Research in Early Childhood' *European Early Childhood Education Research*, vol.19(1), 5–20

Walter J. K. and Ross L. F. (2014) 'Relational Autonomy: Moving Beyond the Limits of Isolated Individualism' *Pediatrics*, vol.133(1), 16–23

Wang, X. (2012) 'The Construction of Researcher-Researched Relationships in School Ethnography: Doing Research, Participating in the Field and Reflecting on Ethical Dilemmas' *International Journal of Qualitative Studies in Education*, vol.26(7), 763–779

Ward, L. (1997) *Seen and Heard: Involving Disabled Children and Young People in Research and Development Projects*, York: York Publishing

Watson, N. (2003) Daily Denials: The Routinisation of Oppression and Resistance, in Riddell, S. and Watson, N. (eds.) *Disability, Culture and Identity: Introduction*, Harlow: Pearson Education Ltd, 34–51

Watson, N., Shakespeare, T., Cunningham-Burley, S. and Barnes, C. (1999) Life as a Disabled Child: A Qualitative Study of Young People's Experiences and Perspectives, Available at: www.esrcsocietytoday.ac.uk [Accessed: 10th November 2013]

Westcott, H. and Littleton, K. S. (2005) Exploring Meaning in Interviews with Children, in Green, S. and Hogan, D. (eds.) *Researching Children's Experience: Approaches and Methods*, London: Sage, 141–157

Wheatley, E. (1994) 'Dances with Feminist: Truth, Dares and Ethnographic Stares' *Women's Studies International Forum*, vol.17(4), 421–423

White, H. (1980) 'The Value of Narrativity in the Representation of Reality' *Critical Inquiry*, vol.7(1), 5–27

Widdicombe, S. and Wooffitt, R. (1995) *The Language of Youth Subcultures: Social Identity in Action*, London: Harvester Wheatsheaf

Wright, K. (2008) 'Researching the Views of Pupils with Multiple and Complex Needs. Is It Worth Doing and Whose Interests Are Served by It?' *Support for Learning*, vol.23(1), 32–40

Young, L. and Barrett, H. (2001) 'Ethics and Participation: Reflections on Research with Street Children' *Ethics, Place and Environment*, vol.4(2), 130–134

Yee, W. C. and Andrews, J. (2006) 'Professional Researcher or a Good Guest? Ethical Dilemmas Involved in Researching Children and Families in the Home Setting' *Education Review*, vol.58(4), 397–413

Yngvesson, B. (2010) *Belonging in an Adopted World*, Chicago: University of Chicago Press

Ytterhus, B. (2012) 'Everyday Segregation Amongst Disabled Children and Their Peers: A Qualitative Longitudinal Study in Norway' *Children and Society*, vol.26, 203–213

Zelizer, V. A. (1985) *Pricing the Priceless Child: The Changing Social Value of Children*, New York: Basic Books

Zignon, J. (2008) *Morality: An Anthropological Perspective*, Oxford: Berg

Zignon, J. (2009) 'Within a Range of Possibilities: Morality and Ethics in Social Life' *Ethnos*, vol.74, 251–276

# Index